Nova Scotia Potluck

YUMMY FOOD
FOR
FRIENDS AND FAMILY

By Shelagh Duffett

With delicious contributions from various friends and family…

Enjoy!

Shelagh Duffett

Cover Credit: Shelagh Duffett

www.DuffettFolkARt.com

Printed in Victoria, Canada.

Note for Librarians: a cataloguing record for this book that includes Dewey Classification and US Library of Congress numbers is available from the National Library of Canada. The complete cataloguing record can be obtained from the National Library's online database at: www.nlc-bnc.ca/amicus/index-e.html

ISBN: 1-4120-2802-7

TRAFFORD

This book was published *on-demand* in cooperation with Trafford Publishing. On-demand publishing is a unique process and service of making a book available for retail sale to the public taking advantage of on-demand manufacturing and Internet marketing. **On-demand publishing** includes promotions, retail sales, manufacturing, order fulfilment, accounting and collecting royalties on behalf of the author.

Suite 6E, 2333 Government St., Victoria, B.C. V8T 4P4, CANADA
Phone   250-383-6864   Toll-free   1-888-232-4444 (Canada & US)
Fax   250-383-6804   E-mail   sales@trafford.com
Web site www.trafford.com   TRAFFORD PUBLISHING IS A DIVISION OF TRAFFORD HOLDINGS, LTD.
Trafford Catalogue # 04-0630   www.trafford.com/robots/04-0630.html

10   9   8   7   6   5   4

Welcome!

I hope you enjoy this little cookbook and reap the benefits of my love for food. I have been wanting to write this book for years, so it gives me great pleasure to finally present you with Nova Scotia Potluck!

I have been collecting recipes for as long as I can remember. These ones have mainly come from friends, gathered at potluck meals! I really enjoy cooking, but it is the end result that motivates me to spend time in the kitchen. Sharing yummy food with kindred souls and family is one of the greatest pleasures I know.

Most of these dishes are easy to make and can either be frozen or made ahead. Important criteria for busy people!

You may notice similar ingredients in these recipes because they are tastes I adore, so, if you like the things I like, you will love this cookbook! Remember, you can substitute low fat ingredients for any of the higher fat ones asked for.

The recipes here aren't "Nova Scotian" as such, but are from people who live here so that makes it a true Nova Scotia Potluck . There are some authentic "Bluenose" recipes to be found within, but they are not the main focus of this cookbook.

The whimsical pictures you see on these pages are my own work. My folk art has been sold all over the world I am happy to think that little pieces of Nova Scotia grace the homes of so many wonderful people! Thanks to all of you who have supported me!

Thanks to all of my friends and family and Bon Appetit to you!

TABLE OF CONTENTS

APPETIZERS

SUPER DUPER FIESTA DIP

*This is one of those layered dishes that has endless variations
and always disappears instantly!*

Base:

1	pkg. 8 oz.	Philadelphia cream cheese, softened	250 gr
8	oz.	sour cream	250 ml
1/2	cup	mayonnaise	125 ml
1	cup	mild salsa sauce	250 ml

Middle:
Approx. 1-2 cups / 250m – 500 ml each diced

green peppers, mushrooms, onions, tomatoes, crumbled bacon,
cooked hamburger, green onions, Jalapenos, black or green
olives, avocado and whatever else might appeal to you.

These are all to your personal taste .Use what you like!

Topping:
1   cup shredded cheddar cheese or more to taste   250 ml

1. Mix together first three ingredients and spread on an
   attractive plate

2. Spread salsa sauce over white mixture.

3. Sprinkle the veggie ingredients in layers on top of the salsa.

4. Top with the cheese and heat until the cheese is melted.
   Big yum!   Serves a large number of happy folk.

KAREN'S INCREDIBLE STUFFED MUSHROOM CAPS

Colleen McNab-These are fabulous ! They can easily be made ahead.

2	large dinner sausages or 4 small sausages	
2	small onions	
1/3	stalk celery	
2	cloves garlic, minced	
30	mushroom caps	
1/4	cup grated mozzarella cheese	50 ml
1/4	cup fine breadcrumbs	50 ml
	salt and pepper	
	crumbled cooked bacon	

1. Remove casings and boil sausage in a bit of water to remove some fat and partially cook.

2. Wash the mushroom caps and set aside in a strainer to dry.

3. Finely chop the onion, celery, garlic and mushroom stems or put in a food processor to chop.

4. Add the veggie mixture to the sausages in the skillet and simmer until sausage is cooked.

5. Add the cheese, breadcrumbs, salt and pepper to taste.

6. Stuff caps with filling and sprinkle with crumbled bacon.

7. Bake for approximately 10 minutes at 400F(200C)
   They can be reheated in the microwave

SUN DRIED TOMATO PESTO ON BRIE

This has all the things I love…. Warm and creamy, it is divine spread on crackers. This is one of those things that can be made up a day ahead or whipped together at the last minute if unexpected guests show up.

2 T	sun dried tomatoes, chopped	30 ml
1 tsp	olive oil	5 ml
2	garlic cloves, minced	
1 tsp.	balsamic vinegar	5 ml
1/4 tsp	basil, dried	1 ml
1/8 cup	parsley, fresh, chopped 25 ml	
pinch	pepper	
1	small brie round	125 gr

1. Cover the tomatoes with boiling water and let stand for 15 minutes to soften. Drain.

2. Heat oil over medium heat in a small frying pan and cook tomatoes, garlic, vinegar and basil for one minute.

3. Remove from the heat and stir in the parsley and pepper.

4. Cut the rind off the top of the Brie cheese.

5. Spread the tomato mixture on top of the Brie. The cheese can be prepared to here and then refrigerated, covered up to one day.

6. Microwave for one minute or bake in a 350F (180C) oven until cheese melts, approx. 10 minutes.

7. Serve immediately surrounded by an assortment of crackers

SOUTHERN COMFORT BAKED BRIE

Sandi Siversky- This was first tasted at a book club meeting one Sunday night and it disappeared in about five minutes! Really yummy.

1	round brie, 8 oz.	225 gr
2 tsp	mango chutney	1 0 ml
1 tsp	dried apricots chopped	5 ml
½ cup	pecan halves	125 ml
2 tsp	honey	10 ml
2 tsp	Southern Comfort, Port, Amarretto or Drambuie	10 ml
1 tsp	balsamic vinegar,	10 ml
	freshly cracked black pepper	

1. Slice the cheese in half

2. Spread middle with chutney and fruit, put back together

3. Arrange nuts on top

4. Mix liquids together and spoon over top

5. Sprinkle with pepper

6. Bake at 375F (190C) for 10 minutes.

7. Serve with an assortment of crackers, or little rounds of French bread

OLIVE PUFFS

These are handy to have on hand if friends drop over unexpectedly or if you are expecting company! Make in advance and keep in the freezer ready to bake at a moment's notice.

1/2 lb.	old cheddar cheese, grated	500gr
1 cup	flour	250 ml
1/2 cup	butter	125 ml
2 tsp.	salt	10 ml
1 jar	stuffed olives, (green manzilla)	
dash	Worcestershire sauce	

1. Mix together the flour, cheese, butter and salt until like dough. The sharper the cheese, the better the flavour of the finished puff.

2. Shape approximately 1 teaspoon of dough around each olive.

3. Bake at 400F (200C) for 12-15 minutes on an ungreased sheet.

4. Can be refrigerated or frozen unbaked. When ready to serve, bring to room temperature and bake.

BLUE CHEESE APRICOTS

Sandi Siversky- Fast and surprisingly tasty. They look great !

12	dried apricots, split almost in half	
1/4 cup	blue cheese	50 ml

1. Fill the apricots with the blue cheese and arrange on an attractive plate!

WARM GARLIC ARTICHOKE DIP

Words cannot describe how yummy this is !!!!!!!!! I could sit down and eat the whole thing with a spoon, forget the crackers!

14oz.	artichoke hearts, drained and finely chopped	400gr
1/2	cup Parmesan cheese (fresh is best)	125ml
1	cup mayonnaise	250 ml
2	cloves finely minced garlic or 1 tsp powder	5 ml
	dash lemon juice	

1. Mix all ingredients together in a heatproof casserole dish

2. Bake at 350F (180C) for 10 to 20 minutes.

Serve with chunks of French bread, crackers or bagel chips.

KILLER GARLIC BREAD

This is a slightly different twist on garlic bread . It is very good.

1	cup mayonnaise	250 ml
1	cup Parmesan cheese, freshly grated	250 ml
2	garlic cloves minced or more if you are brave enough!	
1	pound round sour dough bread halved horizontally	
	(or French bread)	500gr
	butter	
2	Tbsp. fresh basil or 2 tsp. dried	30ml fresh/10 ml dried

1. Preheat broiler

2. Mix together mayonnaise, Parmesan cheese, and garlic in bowl to blend. Set aside.

3. Butter cut side of bread and place on large cookie sheet.

4. Broil until crisp and brown.

5. Spread Parmesan mixture on cut side of bread and broil until puffed and golden.

6. Sprinkle with basil and cut into wedges and serve.

SWEET GARLICKY CHEESE LOG

This is an extremely tasty and irresistible appetizer. The secret ingredient is a brown sugar and mustard coating. People always ask for this recipe!. The best I've ever had. It is an absolute keeper.

8oz.	cream cheese	250 gr.
1 tsp.	garlic, minced (more if you are a garlic fiend)	5 ml
1/3 cup	brown sugar	75 ml
1 tsp.	dry mustard	5 ml
2 tsp.	Worcestershire sauce	10 ml
1/4cup	butter, softened	50 ml
	crushed peanuts or nuts of your choice	

1. Mix together the cream cheese and garlic and form into a log on waxed paper. Refrigerate until firm.

2. Cream together the sugar, butter, dry mustard and Worcestershire sauce and ice the log with this mixture. Place on an attractive plate.

3. Pat the crushed nuts onto the log or roll the log in the nuts.

4. Serve with a knife and heavy crackers.

SALMON PARTY LOG

Moira Langton - One of Moira's favourite appetizers, everyone always looks forward to it at her get togethers. It is attractive, super healthy and is easy to make!.

1	can salmon, drained and deboned	200 gr
8 oz.	cream cheese softened	250 gr
1 Tbsp.	lemon juice	15 ml
2 Tbsp.	onion, grated	30 ml
1 Tbsp.	horseradish or Worcestershire sauce	15 ml
	fresh parsley, chopped	
	pecans or almonds, chopped or whole	

1. Mix everything except the nuts and parsley together.
   *If you want to be a little more health conscious, use the
   low fat cream cheese.

2. Taste and adjust seasonings as desired.

3. Form into log or ball or what ever shape you desire.

4. Roll in chopped parsley and nuts. If nuts are left whole, press
   them into the log.

5. Serve with a knife and crackers or fancy bread.

DEVILLED EGGS

People don't seem to make devilled eggs much any more but every time I put these out on a platter they disappear almost instantly! Use fat free mayonnaise to lower the cholesterol content a wee bit.

6	eggs, large	
2 Tbsp.	mayonnaise	30 ml
2 tsp.	Worcestershire sauce	10 ml
2 Tbsp.	fresh parsley, finely chopped	30 ml
1 tsp.	curry powder	5 ml
	salt and pepper	
	paprika	

1. Cover the eggs in a saucepan with boiling water and simmer for about 11 minutes. Drain and put the eggs in a bowl of cold water to cool or refrigerate overnight.

2. Peel the eggs and cut in half lengthwise. Remove the yolks and place in a small bowl.

3. Mash the yolks with the mayonnaise, Worcestershire, salt, pepper, and parsley(use a fork)

4. Spoon mixture back into the egg whites. Sprinkle with paprika and arrange on a serving platter. Keep cold until serving time. Makes 12

5. For a variation, omit the curry powder and add 1/4 cup (50 ml) of finely diced smoked ham.

HUMMUS

Hummus is a Middle Eastern dip that is becoming quite popular these days. Full of fiber, garlic and lemony goodness. This version is a tasty one! It's a snap to make and keeps well.

1 19 oz. tin	chickpeas, drained and rinsed	540ml
1 Tbsp.	olive oil	15 ml
2 tsp.	salt	10 ml
11/2 tsp.	cumin	7 ml
1-2	garlic cloves, minced	
2 Tbsp.	lemon juice	30 ml
2 Tbsp.	tahini* or peanut butter	30 ml
2 Tbsp.	hot water	30 ml

1. Whiz everything together in a food processor until well blended. Scrape out into an attractive bowl or dish. Add extra water or lemon juice to taste and to get the consistency you want.

2. Garnish with a fresh parlsey sprig, thin lemon slices, a sprinkle of paprika or a small splash of olive oil on the top. Keep in the fridge until serving time. Serve with torn bits of pita bread, melba toast or raw veggies. Keeps for several days.

* Tahini is a sesame seed paste. You can find it in Health food stores, middle Eastern Groceries and probably the health food section in your local supermarket.

CASA CAMERON SALSA

Stewart Cameron-This man grows all his own salsa fixins! A real maestro when it comes to hot and spicy!

3	large red tomatoes, diced	
1	small Spanish onion, minced	
1-2 lg.	cloves garlic, crushed	
2 Tpsp.	fresh cilantro, chopped	30 ml
2 Tbsp.	hot sauce	30 ml
2 Tbsp.	chili sauce	30 ml
1	juice of lime (about 1/4 to 1/2cup)	50 -75 ml
4	hot peppers (Jalapeno or whatever you prefer)	
2	green bell peppers	
	salt	

1. Roast hot peppers and bell peppers under a broiler. You can do this in a toaster oven just until blackened. Put in a zip lock baggie for ten minutes and the skins will slip off. Peel, remove seeds and mince.

2. Mix everything together and season with salt to taste. Adjust to your taste. If you like cilantro, add more!

3. Eat with nacho chips, use with fahitas, or even in an omelette! Ole!

TZATZIKI

This is a Greek cucumber yoghurt dip that I love. It is served with chunks of rustic bread or pita bread and pass me the black olives please! A quick trip to the sunny Greek Isles.

2 cups	plain yoghurt	500 gr
1 cup	cucumber, peeled, seeded, finely grated	250 ml
1 tsp	lemon juice	5 ml
1	garlic clove, minced	
1/2tsp	dill	2 ml

1. Line a sieve with a double thickness of cheesecloth that has been rinsed and squeezed and set over a bowl.

2. Pour the yoghurt into the sieve and let drain for a few hours. It makes the yoghurt lovely and thick.

3. Meanwhile, grate the cucumber and squeeze out the excess moisture.

4. In a bowl, combine all the ingredients and mix well. Add a touch of salt. Cover and chill.

5. Garnish with a dash of paprika, or parsley or a tiny splash of olive oil.

DARK COLA RIBS

Colleen McNab- People will be amazed. Sticky and sweet. Very tasty.

2 pkgs.	pork ribs (about two pounds each)	2kg
2 cans	Cola (12 oz. each)	
1 cup	brown sugar	250 ml
6	garlic cloves, minced	
3 Tbsp.	soya sauce	45 ml

1. Cut ribs into individual pieces. Boil in water for 1 hour. Drain.

2. Add rest of ingredients to pot with ribs.

3. Boil and stir frequently for 40-60 minutes until sauce evaporates, thickens and sticks to ribs. When sauce is sticky thick, it is done!

4. Be careful because it burns very easily.

MAPLE–PEPPER SALMON BITES

These are delicious little bites. They go very well with cold drinks and good company!

1 cup	maple syrup (Nova Scotian is best!!)	250 ml
1/3 cup	soy sauce	75 ml
24 oz.	skinned salmon fillet	650 gr
1/4 cup	black pepper, freshly ground	50 ml
	oil, vegetable or canola	
	sesame seeds toasted(optional)	

1.Cut salmon into bite-size cubes.

2.Combine maple syrup and soy sauce in a medium-size bowl and add salmon, making sure the fish is fully immersed in the marinade. Cover and refrigerate for 24 hours.

3.Grease a sheet of aluminum foil with the oil (vegetable oil sprays work well). Preheat oven to 500F.

4.Put pepper in small bowl or plate and dip top of salmon cubes into cracked black pepper. Be careful not to be too heavy handed.

5. Place each peppered piece on foil, then cook in oven for 3 to 4 minutes. Serve immediately. Sprinkle with sesame seeds if using.

Serves 6 as an appetizer.

HAYLEY'S CALIFORNIA DIP

Hayley Duffett – My daughter said the cookbook wouldn't be complete without her favourite dip so here it is! A very simple classic that has been around for years.

2 cups   sour cream   500 ml
1 pkg.   dry onion soup mix (Lipton's is what we use)

1. Mix the sour cream and soup mix together.

2. Let sit in the fridge for an hour to let the onions soften and the flavours meld.

3. Serve with potato chips or veggie sticks.

4. You can use low fat or no fat sour cream, it is up to you.

SALADS

MARINATED BROCCOLI SALAD

Colleen McNab- This is a great make ahead salad for a potluck. Crunchy and almost sweet and sour. Simple to make. Lots of rave reviews for this one.

1	medium to large broccoli	
1	small to medium red onion	
1	medium to large seeded tomato	
1 cup	flaked almonds, toasted	250 gr
1/4	cup vinegar	50 ml
1/2	cup oil	250ml
1Tbsp.	prepared mustard or more to taste	15 ml
1/8-1/4 cup white sugar		25-50 ml

1. Cut all the veggies into small pieces and put into salad bowl.

2. Mix together oil, vinegar, sugar, and mustard in a small bottle. Shake well to mix.

3. Pour over veggies.

4. Cover with plastic wrap and let sit overnight for flavors to sharpen.

MANDARIN BROCCOLI SALAD

Susan Kirkland - Here is another variation a on a marinated salad. One of those recipes that people always want. Bring this salad to a potluck with some photocopies of the recipe!

4 cups	broccoli flowerettes	1 L
½ cups	raisins	500 ml
½ cups	sliced mushrooms (optional)	500 ml
½ cups	slivered toasted almonds	500 ml
10oz.	mandarin oranges, drained (save the liquid)	284 ml
2	red onion, sliced	
2	eggs	
1 tsp.	cornstarch	10 ml
1/4cup	vinegar	50 ml
1/2cup	mayonnaise	125 ml
1/2cup	sugar	125 ml
1 tsp.	dry mustard	10 ml

1. In a small saucepan, whisk together eggs, sugar, cornstarch, dry mustard.

2. Add vinegar and 1/4 cup(50ml) of mandarin liquid and cook slowly until thickened. (Add water or a little bit of orange juice to make 1/4 cup(50ml) of mandarin liquid if not enough)

3. Remove from heat and stir in the mayonnaise. Cool.

4. Marinate the broccoli in dressing for several hours.

5. Add the remaining ingredients and toss well. Keep in the refrigerator until serving time.

CURRIED SPINACH SALAD

Here is a different twist on spinach salad. It is tart and sweet and satisfying. The chutney tastes better if you have it. This makes a big salad.

2 lb	Spinach, fresh, trimmed, washed and cut into bite sized pieces	1 kg
2/3 cups	peanuts, dry roasted	150 ml
1 ½ -2 cups	raisins	500 ml
¹/2 cups	green onions, sliced thinly	500 ml
2 Tbsp.	sesame seeds, toasted	30 ml
2-3	Red Delicious apples	
¹/2 cups	white wine vinegar	500 ml
2/3cups	salad oil	150 ml
1 Tbsp.	peach chutney or *sweet chili sauce	15 ml
1 tsp.	curry powder	5 ml
1 tsp.	salt	5 ml
1 tsp.	dry mustard powder	5 ml
2 drops	Tabasco sauce (or any hot sauce)	

1. Soak raisins for ten minutes in some apple juice or water to soften up.

2. Prepare spinach, core and dice apples.

3. In a large bowl, toss together the spinach, apples, raisins, peanuts onions and sesame seeds.

4. In a jar, shake all the other ingredients together and pour over the salad.

5. Toss lightly. This makes a big salad. You can halve it for a smaller gathering. You can use ketchup if you have no chili sauce.

LENTIL AND BULGHUR SALAD

Mary Lynass - This is so delicious, it really deserves a better name. Everytime I serve this at a gathering I am asked for the recipe. It makes a large quantity and keeps covered in the fridge for a week but it won't last that long!

1 cup	bulghur wheat	250 ml
19 oz	lentils (canned), drained and rinsed	540 ml
1/4cup	olive oil	50 ml
1/4cup	lemon juice	50 ml
2	cloves garlic, crushed	2
1 tsp.	salt	5 ml
2 Tbsp.	fresh mint (3 tsp dried(15 ml))	30 ml
1-2Tbsp	fresh dill, (2 tsp. dried (10ml))	15- 30 ml
1/4cup	parsley,fresh, minced	50 ml
1/3 cup	green onion, minced	75 ml
1	green or red pepper, small, chopped	1
1/2	stalk celery	
1/2cup	feta, crumbled	125 ml
1/2cup	black olives	125 ml
1	tomato, diced	1
1/2 cup	walnuts or toasted almonds or sunflower seeds, chopped	125 ml
	salt and pepper to taste	

1. First, in medium bowl, soak bulghur in 1 cup (250ml) of boiling water for about ten minutes until bulghur has softened and absorbed most of it. Drain.

2. In large bowl, mix together all of the ingredients. Adjust seasoning.

3. Put it in the fridge for a bit to let the flavours meld. I bet you cannot eat just one spoonful while testing it !

3 BEAN SALAD

Marjorie Tremble - This is one of those salads you can whip up in seconds. A 60's retro salad. It is better the next day, keeps for a long time, is inexpensive to make and is good for you! What more can you ask for!

1 20oz.can	green beans	568 ml
1 20oz.can	yellow beans	568 ml
1 14oz.can	kidney beans	350 ml
2 cups	green pepper (chopped)	500 gr
2 cups	onions, thinly sliced	500 gr
2 cups	vinegar	500 ml
2 cup	salad oil	500 ml
3/4cup	sugar	175 ml
1 tsp.	salt	5 ml
1/4 tsp.	pepper	1 ml

1. Drain all the beans. (Rinse the kidney beans.)

2. Mix everything together in an attractive bowl and serve! This keeps well in the fridge. You can make ahead and let marinate if you want.

ORIENTAL RICE SALAD

The textures in this salad are great. Crunchy, smooth and silky. Another yummy hit! It travels well and is better the next day. If making in advance, put the peanuts on just before serving.

5 cups	cooked rice, (brown gives best texture)	1250 ml
2	green onions, thinly sliced	
1	large carrot, finely chopped	
1	celery stalk, finely chopped	
1 cup	water chestnuts, thinly sliced	250 ml
1 cup	red bell pepper, finely chopped	250 ml
2 cups	chopped peanuts	250 gr
2 1/2Tbsp.	peanut butter, smooth or chunky	38 ml
1 tsp.	fresh ginger, finely chopped or grated	5 ml
1/3 cup.	olive oil or salad oil	75 ml
3 Tbsp.	red wine vinegar	45 ml
1 1/2Tbsp.	sesame oil*	22 ml
	salt and pepper to taste	

1. Make the dressing. In a small bowl, mix together the peanut butter and the ginger. Stir in the oils, vinegar, salt and pepper until smooth. Taste and adjust the seasonings as desired.

2. In a large mixing bowl, put in the rice and break up any large chunks. Add the rest of the ingredients except the peanuts and mix well.

3. Pour the dressing over the salad and mix until everything is coated.

4. Mound the rice in a serving bowl and sprinkle the nuts over the top.

*Available in specialty section of grocery store

31

MANDARIN AND PINEAPPLE SALAD

Kathy McNab - Light and fluffy.. Something different to bring to the potluck table.

1	package orange Jello powder	
1	can mandarin oranges, drained (10 oz)	284 ml
1	can pineapple cubes, drained (10 0z)	284 ml
2 cups	cottage cheese	500 ml
11/2	cups Cool Whip	375 ml

1. Mix everything together in a bowl and put in the fridge to cool and firm. May be made in a mold. (lightly grease first.)

TOASTED SESAME SALAD DRESSING

Carolyn Bourque- Serve this over a mixed spinach and romaine salad with sliced apple, mandarin oranges, or strawberries.

1 Tbsp.	sesame seeds, toasted *	15 ml
1/4cup	cider vinegar	50 ml
3 Tbsp.	oil	45 ml
3 Tbsp.	water	45 ml
1 Tbsp.	brown sugar (or white)	15 ml
1 tsp.	poppy seeds	5 ml
1/4tsp.	paprika	1 ml
1/4 tsp.	Worcestershire sauce	1 ml
1	green onion , minced	

1. Whisk all the ingredients together and pour over salad.

2. Serve over fresh spinach with sliced strawberries and toasted almonds.

   To toast sesame seeds, put into an ungreased pan over medium-high heat and stir until lightly brown

CRANBERRY FETA GREENS SALAD

Green, red and white make this salad wonderful to look at. The taste is bright and tangy sweet. A really festive salad.

2 cups	lettuce, torn into bite sized pieces	500 gr
2 cups	spinach, torn into bite sized pieces	500 gr
8 Tbsp.	cranberries, dried (craisins)	120 ml
8 Tbsp.	feta cheese, crumbled	120 ml
1	Bermuda onion or red onion, finely chopped	
1/2cup	hazelnuts or almonds, toasted and chopped	
	(optional)	75 ml
1 1/2 cups	canola oil	375 ml
1/2 cups	apple cider vinegar	
1/2 cup	lemon juice	125 ml
1 tsp.	salt	10 ml
1 tsp.	dry mustard	10 ml
1 tsp.	paprika	10 ml
1/3 cup	honey	75 ml

1. In a jar with a lid, add together the oil, vinegar, lemon juice, salt, mustard, paprika and honey. (Taste and adjust honey.)

2. Shake well to mix. Refrigerate until ready to use.

3. In a large bowl, toss together the lettuce and spinach.

4. Scatter the crumbled feta, cranberries, nuts(if using) and onion on top.

5. Drizzle the dressing over all and toss before serving.

PINE NUT PASTA SALAD

Moira Langton - Ever have a hard time finding something that everyone in the family loves? Well, Moira made this one night and it disappeared before her eyes! The textures are nice. Adjust the ingredients to what suits you, less olives, more parsley? More lemon juice, less peppers?

2 cups	pine nuts	500 ml
2 Tbsp.	butter	30 ml
2 lbs.	alphabet pasta or any small pasta shape	900 gr
2 cups	parsley, fresh, minced	500 ml
1 cup	black olives	250 ml
2 cups	green onion, minced	500 ml
1/3 cup	green bell pepper, diced	75 ml
1/3 cup	red bell pepper, diced	75 ml
1/ 4cup	lemon juice (fresh is best)	50 ml
1/ 4cup	olive oil	50 ml
	black pepper, ground	
	Parmesan cheese, to taste	

1. In large frying pan melt the butter and lightly toast the pine nuts. Drain and cool.

2. Cook pasta in boiling water till soft. (Don't over cook.) Drain and rinse in cold water.

3. Gently mix everything together.

4. Cover and chill. Top with Parmesan cheese and ground pepper. Serves 6.

EGGLESS CAESAR SALAD

This recipe does not use a raw egg in the dressing and is just as good. It is really garlicky so if you are faint of heart, put one or two less cloves in. Sour cream is the secret to the creaminess.

2-3	lg. garlic cloves, minced, mashed to a paste with a pinch of salt	
2 Tbsp.	lemon juice, fresh	30 ml
1 Tbsp.	Worcestershire sauce	15ml
1 tsp.	Dijon mustard	5 ml
4 Tbsp.	sour cream	60 ml
1/4 tsp.	ground pepper, freshly ground (to taste)	1 ml
3	anchovy fillets (or 1Tbsp. paste from tube)	15 ml
1 1/2 cups	olive oil	375 ml
1/3 cup	Parmesan cheese, freshly grated	75 ml
8 cups	packed bite-sized pieces of Romaine lettuce, rinsed and spun dry.	2L
	croutons to taste	

1. In large salad bowl, stir together the garlic paste, lemon juice, Worcestershire sauce, mustard, sour cream, pepper and anchovies.

2. Add the oil in a stream, whisking constantly and keep whisking until the salad dressing has incorporated all the oil and is emulsified.

3. Stir in the Parmesan cheese, add the lettuce and toss the salad well. Top with croutons if you are so inclined. Serves 4.

HONG KONG NAPPA SALAD

Jackie Glinsky - This serves a huge crowd but can be halved for a family. It can also be made ahead and kept refrigerated. Just what we like!

2 pkgs.	Ramen Noodles (those dried small packages of Oriental soup noodles)	
1 large	nappa cabbage, shredded	
2 cups	parsley, fresh,chopped	500 ml
8	green onions, chopped	
1 cup	toasted almonds, chopped	250 ml
1/2cup	sunflower seeds, toasted	125 ml
3/4 cup	salad oil	175 ml
6 Tbsp.	vinegar	90 ml
4 tsp.	white sugar	20 ml
2 tsp.	salt	10 ml
2	seasoning packets from Ramen Noodles garlic powder, if desired	

1. In a jar with a lid, mix together the oil, sugar, vinegar, salt and seasoning packets. (Add garlic if wanted)

2. In a large bowl, toss together the rest of the ingredients.

3. Pour over the dressing and mix well.

4. Cover and refrigerate.

SPINACH SALAD WITH MAPLE DRESSING

Kathy Greenwood - Yum. The first time Kathy served this, everyone wanted to know what was in the dressing. The maple syrup gives it a delightful sweetness. There are never any leftovers and the bowl is always cleaned out! Another one of those recipes people always ask for.

10 oz.	spinach, torn into bite sized bits	284 ml
3	bacon strips crisp and crumbled	
1	apple, unpeeled and diced	
1/4 cup	cheddar cheese, grated	50 ml
1/4 cup	mozzerella cheese, grated	50 ml
3/4 cup	mayonnaise	175 ml
1 Tbsp.	lemon juice	15 ml
1 tsp.	vinegar	10 ml
1/2 cup	sugar	125 ml
3 Tbsp.	maple syrup (Nova Scotian of course!)	45 ml
	fresh parsley, chopped	

1. Wash and dry the spinach and tear into small pieces.

2. In large serving bowl, mix together the spinach, bacon, apple, and cheeses.

3. In a container with a lid, mix together the mayonnaise, lemon juice, vinegar, sugar, and maple syrup.

4. Pour dressing over the spinach salad and toss together.

5. Sprinkle the parsley over the top.

CRUNCHY CHICKEN AND PINEAPPLE SALAD

Very easy to make and addictive to eat. This will serve four normal people or two addicts! If you want to be really fancy, serve in hollowed out pineapple boats surrounded by fresh strawberries and greens. WOW This salad is easily doubled.

3 cups	cooked chicken, chopped coarsely (1lb)	500 gr
1 cup	celery, chopped	250 ml
½ -1 cup	slivered almonds or pecans, toasted	250 ml
½ cup	fresh pineapple chunks	125 ml
½ cup	halved red grapes (optional) or can be used instead of pineapple	125 ml
½ cup	mayonnaise (low fat ok, but not as yummy)	125 ml
2 Tbsp.	lemon juice	30 ml
2 Tbsp.	chopped fresh parsley	30 ml
	salt and pepper	

1. In a large bowl, combine chicken, celery, nuts, pineapple, grapes (if using), mayonnaise and lemon juice. Season with salt and pepper.

2. Toss to blend thoroughly. Serve chilled on lettuce leaves or as I mentioned above, in hollowed out pinepapple halves!!

3. For a different twist you can add 2Tbsp. finely chopped, crystallized ginger to the mixture. Serves 4

SPICY ASIAN STYLE PASTA SALAD

This can be a side dish or add some cooked chicken or shrimp to turn it into the main fare! It is a terrific dish to take to any potluck affair. People love it.

1 lb	linguine, broken in half or rotini	500gr
4 Tbsp.	oriental sesame oil	60 ml
3 Tbsp.	honey	45 ml
3 Tbsp	soy sauce	45 ml
3 Tbsp.	balsamic vinegar	45 ml
1/4 tsp.	cayenne pepper	1 ml
3	red or green bell peppers, seeded, thinly sliced	
3 cups	snow peas	750 ml
1	large red onion, thinly sliced or green onions	
3/4cup	honey-roasted peanuts, coarsely chopped or cashews or pecans or almonds	175 ml
1/2cup	fresh basil or cilantro, chopped	125 ml

1. Cook pasta in large pot of boiling salted water until tender but still firm to bite, stirring occasionally. Drain very well. Transfer to large bowl.

2. Whisk 3 tablespoons sesame oil, honey, soy sauce, vinegar and cayenne pepper in small bowl to blend. Season with salt.

3 . Mix half of dressing into pasta.

4. Heat remaining 1 tablespoon oil in heavy large pot over medium-high heat. Add bell peppers, peas and onion and saute until just beginning to wilt, about 2 minutes.

5. Add vegetables to pasta. Mix in nuts, basil and enough dressing to coat. Serve, passing any remaining dressing separately. Delicious! Serves 6.

ROMAINE AND MANDARIN SALAD

This used to be the salad I made for every occasion. It is light tasting and satisfyingly yummy. I have given this recipe out to many people. I must start making it again!

1 head	romaine lettuce, washed and torn	
1/2 cup	sunflower seeds	125 ml
1/2 cup	almonds, sliced	125 ml
2 Tbsp	butter	30 ml
2	green onions, chopped	
10 oz	mandarin oranges, drained	284 ml
1/2cup	oil	125 ml
3Tbsp.	red wine vinegar	45 ml
1Tbsp	lemon juice	15 ml
2 tsp.	sugar	10 ml
1/2 tsp	salt	2 ml
1/2 tsp	dry mustard	2 ml
1	garlic clove, crushed	
	avocado, optional	

1. Heat butter in a frying pan and gently fry the sunflowers and almonds until golden brown colour. If you want, you can add a tablespoon of brown sugar and caramelize them a bit. Cool.

2. Combine the oil, vinegar, lemon juice, sugar, garlic, mustard and salt in a jar and shake.

3. In large bowl, put in lettuce, top with green onions and nuts.

4. Toss with dressing just before serving. Garnish with avocado slices.

MORROCAN COUS COUS SALAD

Anna Migas - This is sooo good. Uses up the veggies in your fridge. Feel free to play with this...add more carrot, chick peas, lemon. Fluffing the cous cous is critical otherwise it will be lumpy and pasty.

2 cups	chicken/veggie stock	500 ml
3/4 tsp	cinnamon	3 ml
1/2 tsp	ginger	2 ml
1/2 tsp	cumin	2 ml
1/4 tsp	turmeric	1 ml
1 cup	cous cous	250 ml
1	carrot, 1/4 " diced	
1	red pepper, 1/4" diced	
1/2	english cuke 1/4" diced	
1	red onion, finely minced	
1	Granny Smith apple, diced finely	
1/3 cup	currants	75 ml
1 cup	chick peas	250 ml
1/4 cup	lemon juice	50 ml
	salt and pepper	
3 Tbsp	olive oil	45 ml

1. In a medium saucepan, add the spices to the stock and bring to a boil. Add the cous cous. Take off heat.

2. Let sit covered for 5 minutes. Fluff up (with 2 forks) and cool.

3. Add the rest of the ingredients to the cous cous and mix well. Adjust seasonings and put into an attractive bowl.

SOUPS

NOVA SCOTIA SEAFOOD CHOWDER

Cathy Cameron- One bowlful and all your worries melt away. On the day I borrowed this recipe, no sooner had I arrived home than the phone rang and it was Cathy asking if I had the chowder recipe near by. Her mother in law had just called looking for it. Well, here it is for all to share and it is even better on day two. It makes enough for a dozen people!

6 cups	water	1.5L
4	large potatoes, diced	
1	large onion, diced	
1 tsp.	salt	5 ml
1 lb.	raw fish (haddock, sole, pollock, salmon or chowder mix)	500 gr
1 1/4cups	canned lobster, broken	300 ml
10 oz.	can clams	284 ml
12 oz.	scallops	300 ml
2 cups	cereal cream	500 ml
1 cup	whole milk	250 ml
4 Tbsp	butter	60 ml
½ tsp	pepper	2 ml
2-3 Tbsp	fresh parsley, chopped (1Tbsp. if dried)	30 ml
¼ cup	green onion (chopped)	50 ml

1. Simmer potatoes in water in large pot until tender. Add onion, fish and salt.

2. Simmer until fish is tender, and toss in rest of seafood. Cook gently for five minutes.

3. Add cream milk and butter, heat until hot but not boiling, simmer very gently on low heat for 20 minutes.

4. Adjust seasonings, add parsley and green onion.

DREAM OF TOMATO SOUP

Hazel McNab- This is one of those soups you could get addicted to. It is tart and savory and cheesy. I have given this recipe to many!

2 cans	tomatoes, (19oz) chopped	1080 ml
1 lg.	onion, finely chopped	
1 cup	celery, chopped	250 ml
10oz.	chicken broth (one can)	284 ml
1/2 cup	spicy Clamato juice	125 ml
1 Tbsp	dill weed	15 ml
1/4 cup	butter	50 ml
1/4 -1/2cup	flour	50 -75 ml
4 cups	milk	1 L
1 cup	Cheese Whiz (not the healthiest of ingredients but so essential to this soup!)	250 ml
	parsley for garnish	

1. Simmer tomatoes, onions, celery, broth, dill and Clamato juice till veggies are tender, about 20 minutes.

2. In large saucepan, make a white sauce. (Melt butter, stir in flour, add milk slowly while stirring).

3. Stir in veggie mixture slowly and then fold in the Cheese Whiz.

4. Garnish with parsley . Serves 14-16. Freezes well.

CABBAGE AND POTATO SOUP

Talk about good for what ails you! A Nova Scotian, South shore specialty. A soup guaranteed to chase away the blues.

3 cups	chicken broth	750 ml
2 cups	shredded cabbage	500 ml
2 med.	potatoes, pared & diced (about 1 lb.)	500 gr
2 Tbsp.	butter	30 ml
1 cup	chopped leeks (or any green onion)	250 ml
3 Tbsp.	all purpose flour	45 ml
1½ cups	Half and half, divided (or *blend milk)	375 ml
2 tsp.	Dijon-style mustard	10 ml
¾ tsp.	Worcestershire sauce	3 ml
½ tsp.	caraway seed	2 ml
¼ tsp.	pepper	1 ml
2-3 drops	Tabasco sauce	
½ cup	bacon, crisply cooked and crumbled (optional)	75 ml

1 .In a large saucepan, heat broth over medium heat. Add cabbage and potatoes. Cover and simmer about 15 minutes until potatoes are tender.

2. In a large skillet, over medium-high heat, melt butter. Add leeks and cook until tender. Stir in flour and cook 2 or 3 minutes.

3. Add 1 cup half and half to the broth mixture. Add leeks. Add remaining ingredients, stir in remaining half and half. Cook over low heat 10 to 15 minutes.

4.Top bowls with crumbled bacon

NOVA SCOTIA VEGETABLE HODGE PODGE

My mum and dad would make this on a Saturday morning and enjoy it throughout the weekend. It is a classic vegetable chowder particular to this province. I just love it..You use six cups of any vegetables you have on hand. I will give you the ones we use.

1 cup	baby carrots	250 ml
1 cup	small new potatoes	250 ml
1 cup	green beans	250 ml
1 cup	broccoli	250 ml
1 cup	snow peas	250 ml
1 cup	shelled peas or frozen will do	250 ml
1	large onion, chopped	
1Tbsp.	butter	15 ml
1 Tbsp.	fresh parsley, chopped	15 ml
1 cup	whole milk or cream	250 ml

1. Cut veggies into 1 inch (2.5cm) pieces approximately.

2. Fry onion in 1Tbsp of butter until golden, set aside

3. In pot, cook veggies in 2 cups (500ml) water till tender. Start with potatoes and carrots and add the rest.

4. When the veggies are cooked, pour off the water, saving 1/4 cup (50 ml) of the veggie broth.

5. Add the onions to the veggies and 1/4 cup broth and add the milk. Heat gently, Do NOT BOIL, Sprinkle with fresh parsley and ground pepper.

CECILE'S RED LENTIL SOUP

Cecile Leverman -This soup has very little fat, is cheap and easy to make and delicious. Their family practically lives on it in the winter and she usually doubles the recipe. Sprinkle grated cheddar on top if you wish. If you can't hang around long enough for this to cook, put it in a slow cooker

1/2 cup	red or green lentils	125 ml
1 cup	chopped onion	250 ml
1	stalk celery, chopped	
2 cups	shredded cabbage or other veggies	500 ml
28 oz	tomatoes (canned) chopped	818 ml
2 cups	chicken broth	500 ml
3	carrots, chopped	
2	cloves garlic, crushed	
1 tsp	salt	5 ml
1/2 tsp	ground black pepper	2 ml
1/4tsp	white sugar	1 ml
1/2 tsp	dried basil	2 ml
1 tsp	dried thyme	5 ml
1/4tsp	curry powder	1 ml

1. Place the lentils into a stockpot or a Dutch oven and add water to twice the depth of the lentils . Bring to a boil, then lower heat and let simmer for about 15 minutes. Drain and rinse lentils; return them to the pot.

2. Add onion, celery, cabbage/veggies, tomatoes, chicken broth, carrots and garlic to the pot and season with salt, pepper, sugar, basil, thyme and curry. Cook, simmering for 1 1/2 to 2 hours or until desired tenderness is achieved. If too thick add more stock or water..

3. Serve with grated cheese. Makes 6 –1cup (250 ml) servings.

BUTTERNUT SQUASH AND APPLE SOUP

This has a lovely texture and is beautiful to look at. It is packed with nutritional goodness and tastes wonderful too. It is one of my favorites.

1 Tbsp.	butter	15 ml
2	cloves garlic	2
1	onion, chopped	1
1 tsp.	curry powder	5 ml
1 1/2 lbs	squash, cut into 1" pieces (approx 4 cups)	750 gr
1	Granny Smith apple, or other tart apple, chopped	
1/2 cups	chicken broth	500 ml
1 1/2cups	milk	375 ml
	salt and pepper to taste	

1. In a heavy saucepan, fry the onion and garlic until soft.

2. Add curry powder, squash, apple and chicken broth, simmer, covered, until squash is tender, 15 minutes or so.

3. In a blender, puree mixture in batches until smooth.OR if you have a hand blender, you can use that in the pot itself.

4. Return soup to pot and add milk. Add 1 cup (250 ml) of the milk and check the consistency, if too thick, add more. Add salt and pepper to taste. Reheat gently, do not boil.

5. Serve topped with crumbled bacon, or finely minced green onion

PIZZA SOUP

Linda MacNeil- This tastes just like the real thing! Kids love it. Terrific after a day outside being busy. Serve with crusty French bread.

1 Tbsp.	olive oil	15 ml
1	onion, chopped	
½ cup	mushrooms, fresh, sliced	125 ml
¼ cup	green pepper, slivered	50 ml
28 oz	plum tomatoes (canned) chopped, undrained	796 gr
1 cup	beef stock	250 ml
1 cup	pepperoni or salami, thinly sliced	250 ml
½ tsp	basil, dried, or more to taste	3 ml
2 cups	mozzerella cheese, shredded	500 ml

1. In large saucepan, over medium heat, fry onion, mushrooms and green pepper until soft, but not brown.

2. Add the tomatoes, beef stock, pepperoni and basil. Cook until just to the boiling point.

3. Ladle into 4 ovenproof bowls. Sprinkle with cheese. Broil under grill until cheese melts and is bubbly OR microwave on high for 1 minute.

4. If you don't have a microwave or ovenproof bowls, it is just fine with the cheese sprinkled on top too.

HAMBURGER SOUP

This soup is a hearty meal in itself! Cook it in a crock pot to really make things easy for yourself. It is the perfect soup to take over to new mom, a new neighbor, someone who is not feeling well or even just because! This freezes well.

11/2 lb	hamburger, lean	570 gr
1	onion, medium, chopped	
28 oz.	tomatoes (canned) chopped,	796 ml
3 cans	consommé(10 oz)	3 x 284 ml
2 cans	tomato soup(10oz) low sodium if possible	2 x 284 ml
2 cans	water (10 oz)	500 ml
3	carrots, chopped	
4	stalks, celery, chopped	
½ cup	barley	125 ml
½ tsp	thyme	3 ml
1 tsp	basil	3 ml
2 tsp	parsley	10 ml
1	bayleaf	
1 tsp.	Worcestershire sauce, optional	5ml

1. In frying pan, brown the hamburger and the onion until the meat is no longer pink. Drain the fat.

2. Put all the ingredients together in a large crockpot and cook all day or in a very large pot on the stove covered for 2 hours. It makes a lot!. Freezes well.

SIDE DISHES

HASH BROWN POTATO CASSEROLE

Pam Noseworthy- Pam is absolutely one of the best cooks I know. We have spent many happy hours in the past discussing food as well as eating it! This is one of her standards for a crowd. It freezes well and is simple to make. Serves 8.

2 lbs.	frozen hash brown potatoes (one bag)	1kg
1 cup	onion, finely chopped	250 ml
2 cups	sour cream (you can use low fat if desired)	500 ml
1 lb	old cheddar cheese, grated	500 gr
2	cans Cream of Mushroom or Cream of Chicken Soup (undiluted)	568 ml
1/2	soup can water (15 oz)	140 ml
1/4 lb	butter, melted	250 gr
1 tsp	garlic powder or more to taste	5 ml
	salt and pepper	
	crushed potato chips or corn flakes (optional)	

1. Thaw the hash browns for 30 minutes.

2. Mix everything together in a greased 9X13 (3.5L) dish except the potato chips. If you like you can use a large bowl and then transfer to the baking dish.

3. Sprinkle with the crushed chips and or corn flakes and bake uncovered at 350 F(180C) for one hour.

4. You can cover and refrigerate for a day or freeze before cooking. Remove 2 hours before baking and sprinkle with crushed chips.(optional)

CELTIC COLCANNON

A classic Irish dish, this is soul food for the Brits.. I love the combination of potatoes, cabbage, onion and bacon. Makes 8 servings.

2 1/2 lbs	potatoes, peeled and cubed	1kg
5	slices bacon	
1/2	small head cabbage, chopped (3 cups approx.)	750 ml
1	large onion, chopped	
1/2 cup	milk	125 ml
	salt and pepper to taste	
1/4 cup	butter, melted	50 ml

1. Place potatoes in a saucepan with enough water to cover. Bring to a boil, cook for 15 to 20 minutes, until tender.

2. In a large deep frying pan, cook bacon over medium high heat until evenly brown, not totally crispy. Drain, reserving drippings, crumble and set aside.

4. In the reserved drippings, fry the cabbage and onion until soft and translucent. Putting a lid on the pan helps speed the cooking.

5 Drain the cooked potatoes, mash with milk and season with salt and pepper. Fold in the bacon, cabbage, and onions.

6. Transfer the mixture to a large serving bowl. Make a well in the center, and pour in the melted butter. Serve immediately.

MIMI'S DEVILLED CORN

Pam Noseworthy- This is a delicious addition to any table! Mimi, Pam's mother-in-law made this often I just love it. Don't be put off by the long list of ingredients. It is easy to make.

4Tbsp.	butter	60 ml
2 Tbsp.	flour	30 ml
1 Tbsp.	lemon juice	15 ml
1/2 cup	milk	125 ml
14oz	corn niblets	400 ml
1/2 cup	Parmesan cheese	125 ml
1 Tbsp.	butter, melted	15 ml
2	hard-boiled eggs	2
1 tsp.	dry mustard	5 ml
1/2 tsp	salt	2 ml
3 slices	bacon, cooked, crumbled	3
14oz	creamed corn	400 ml
1/2cup	cracker crumbs	125 ml
2	hard-boiled eggs, sliced	2

1. Melt 4 Tbsp.butter (60ml) and add flour, mustard, lemon juice and salt.

2. Add milk and stir until thickened. Remove from heat, add bacon, chopped eggs, and both tins of corn.

3. Put into a greased casserole dish and sprinkle with Parmesan cheese. Combine the melted butter and breadcrumb and sprinkle over the cheese.

4. Bake at 350F (180C) for 45 minutes. Add a garnish of sliced eggs and chopped green olives if desired. Serves 6

CURRIED FRUIT

Hazel McNab - This is a nice addition to the potluck table. It is sweet and savory, good hot or cold and can be made in advance. You can vary the fruit you use according to what is available to you This keeps well for several days.

1/3 cup	butter	75 ml
1/3cup	brown sugar	75 ml
1-2Tbsp.	curry powder	15-30 ml
16oz.	pear halves	500 ml
16oz.	peach halves	500 ml
16oz.	pineapple slices	500 ml
16oz.	apricot halves	500 ml

1. Melt butter in saucepan or microwave, add sugar and curry powder and mix well.

2. Drain fruits slightly and arrange in a casserole dish. Top with curry mixture.

3. Bake for 1 hour at 350F (180C).

GREEN BEANS WITH PEANUT SAUCE

What a versatile dish this is! It is tasty hot or cold and can be made ahead to let the flavours meld. Great on a buffet table.

1 lb.	green beans, trimmed ends and cut in half	500gr
1/2 cup	peanut butter, smooth or chunky	125 ml
1 Tbsp.	dark brown sugar, packed	15 ml
1 Tbsp.	soy sauce	15 ml
1 Tbsp.	lemon juice	15 ml
1 lg.	garlic clove, minced	
2-3	slices of fresh ginger	
1/2 cups	hot water	500 ml
	sesame seeds (optional)	

1. Cook the beans in lightly salted boiling water until tender, about 5 minutes. Drain and rinse under cold water.

2. In a food processor, combine the peanut butter, sugar, soy sauce, lemon juice, garlic and ginger. Process until smooth Add the hot water while the machine is running and blend until well mixed.

3. Arrange the beans in an attractive serving dish and pour the sauce over. If you would like the dish warm, microwave on high for 50 seconds, turning once. Sprinkle with sesame seeds for a pretty finish.

4. If you are not going to serve it serve right away, cover and refrigerate.

CHICK PEAS WITH GARLIC AND ROSEMARY

This can be doubled easily. Take your guests to the south of France with this tasty and healthy salad.

19oz.	can chick peas or 2 cups cooked	540 ml
1/2 cup	water	125 ml
2	garlic cloves, peeled and finely minced	
1 tsp	dried rosemary or 2 sprigs fresh	5 ml
1cup	tomatoes, chopped	250 ml
1Tbsp.	red wine vinegar	15 ml
2Tbsp.	olive oil	30 ml
	salt and pepper	
	fresh Italian parsley, chopped	

1. Empty chick peas into a saucepan with their juice and add water, garlic, and rosemary.

2. Bring to a boil, reduce heat and simmer for 15 minutes.

3. Drain liquid and discard rosemary sprig if fresh was used.

4. Add tomatoes and cook 5 minutes to reduce sauce a bit.

5. Add oil, vinegar, salt and pepper.

6. Garnish with parsley. Can be served hot, room temperature or cold. Serves 4.

KALE WITH SAUTEED APPLE AND ONION

2	Granny Smith apples	
4 Tbsp	olive oil	60 ml
2	onions, medium, cut into 1/4-inch wedges	
1 tsp	curry powder(1/2 tsp if less spice wanted)	2-5 ml
2 lbs	kale, tough stems and ribs removed and leaves coarsely chopped	1 kg
1 cup	water or chicken broth (broth is tastier)	250 ml
	cooked crumbled bacon or finely chopped cooked ham (optional for garnish)	

1. Peel, quarter, and core apple, then cut into 1/4-inch-thick wedges.

2. Heat oil in a large pot over moderately high heat until hot but not smoking, then fry the onion, stirring occasionally, until golden.

3. Add apple and curry powder and fry, stirring, until apple is almost tender, about 2 minutes.

4. Add kale and water or broth and cook, covered, stirring occasionally, until kale is tender and most of liquid is evaporated, about 5 minutes.

5. Season with salt and top with a bit of crumbled bacon or finely chopped cooked ham if using. Makes 4 servings.

JANET'S SCALLOPED POTATOES

Cecile Leverman -These are different from the usual scalloped potatoes in that they have carrots and cheese in them. They are really good! The first time Cecile tasted them she had to have the recipe and now it is ours too.

6 large	potatoes, sliced	
5	carrots, sliced	
1 1/2 cups	onion, sliced	375 ml
2Tbsp	butter	30 ml
2Tbsp	flour	30 ml
1 1/2cups	milk	375 ml
1Tbsp	salt	15 ml
1 1/2 cups	cheddar cheese, shredded(old is best)	375 ml
	black pepper to taste	

1. In a pot of salted water, boil together the potatoes, carrots and onion for 5 minutes. Preheat the oven to 350F (180C).

2. Drain the potatoes and put the mixture in a 9x13" (3.5L) pan.

3. In a saucepan over medium heat, melt the butter and then add the flour to make a paste. Sprinkle in some pepper to taste. Slowly add the milk stirring all the while until smooth and thickened. Then add the cheese and stir until melted.

4. Pour the sauce over the potato mixture. Cover with foil and bake at 350F (180C) for 40 minutes.

5. If desired, take out of oven, sprinkle with some extra cheese and put back uncovered for another 5 minutes.

INDIAN SPICED CABBAGE

Pam Noseworthy –I could eat a whole cabbage cooked like this! Pam got this recipe from an Indian friend of hers and it has now become a staple in our house any time we cook East Indian or want something different on our potluck table.

1	cabbage, shredded finely	
1/3 tsp.	cumin	2 ml
2 tsp.	salt	10 ml
1 1/2 tsp.	tumeric	7 ml
2 tsp.	chili powder	10 ml
2 tsp.	garam masala (find in specialty section of grocery store)	10 ml
2 tsp.	black pepper	10 ml

1. In a large pot, heat oil to cover bottom of pot 1/4" to 1/2" (1/2cm -1cm).

2. Add cumin and cook 30 seconds. It will sizzle and pop and smell wonderful.

3. Add rest of spices and then add cabbage.

4. Stir to coat cabbage with oil and spices.

5. Cover and cook on medium until cabbage soft. Approximately 2 hours.

6. Serve in a large colorful bowl.

CHEDDAR BROCCOLI CASSEROLE

Hazel McNab- One word, yummy!

1 cup	onion, finely chopped	250 ml
1 cup	mushrooms, sliced	250 ml
1 large	broccoli head,cut up	
10oz.	can Cream of Mushroom soup	284 ml
1/4lb.	cheddar cheese, grated	125 gr
2 tsp.	garlic powder or 2 cloves minced	10 ml
3/4cup	almonds, sliced	150 ml

1. In saucepan, fry onions and mushrooms in a bit of butter till onions are soft.

2. Add soup, garlic and cheese and stir over low heat until cheese melts.

3. Cut up broccoli and cook briefly in boiling water (5min.)

4. Drain and add to sauce.

5. Add almonds saving some for the top.

6. Pour into a casserole dish and top with breadcrumbs and remaining almonds.

7. Bake for 30 minutes at 350F (180C).

BUTTERY MAPLE CARROTS

Need I say more?

3 cups	carrots, sliced	750 ml
2 Tbsp.	butter	30 ml
1/4cup	maple syrup	50 ml
1 tsp.	lemon juice	5 ml
1/2 tsp.	salt	2 ml

1. Cook carrots until just tender

2. Melt the butter in a separate sauce pan and add the maple syrup, lemon juice and salt. Bring to a boil and pour over drained carrots.

TANGY ORANGE SWEET POTATOES

Marmalade is the ingredient that makes this a bit different.

2	sweet potatoes, medium sized or 19 oz can	540 ml
2 Tbsp.	marmalade	30 ml
1 Tbsp	butter	15 ml
	black pepper to taste	

1. Cook sweet potatoes until soft and mash

2. Add the marmalade and butter and a pinch of pepper.

3. Scoop into a pretty bowl and serve.

4. If using the canned sweet potato, mix all ingredients together and cook in a 350F (180C) oven for 15 minutes or until hot.

RATATOUILLE

This is a great way to get in some extra veggies. My dad loved this dish. It is a recipe from Provence in France and full of the flavours of sunny days. It is good warm or cold.

3 Tbsp	olive oil	45 ml
2	onions, chopped in chunks	
4-5	cloves of garlic, smashed	
28 oz	tomatoes (canned) chopped up	796 ml
1	eggplant, medium, cut into small chunks, 1/2- 3/4"	2cm
2	zucchini, medium, cut into small chunks, 1/2-3/4"	2cm
1	green pepper, sliced	
1	red pepper, sliced	
2 Tbsp	basil, fresh, chopped	30 ml
2 Tbsp	Italian parsley.or regular, fresh, chopped	30 ml
1 tsp	salt and pepper to taste	5 ml

1. In a large heavy saucepan, over medium heat, cook onions and garlic in oil until softened but not brown.

2. Add tomatoes with juice, and cook till thickened, about 5 minutes.

3. Add the rest of the veggies and cook until tender about 20 minutes.

4. Add the herbs, salt and pepper to taste. You can serve this now, wait till until it is room temperature or eat cold. I prefer it at room temperature.

5. This is delicious as an omelette filling, on pasta or by itself as an accompaniment to any meal.

**You can substitute 3 fresh tomatoes chopped, and roast all the ingredients at 400F(200c) for 45 minutes in a shallow pan Stirring occasionally.

MAIN COURSES

FETTUCINE AND HAM CASSEROLE

Make this the day before and bake it when you need it. This can also be made with all low fat ingredients for a lighter dish if desired. Serve with a crisp green salad and some sliced tomatoes.

8 oz.	fettucine, uncooked	250 gr
1/2 lb.	cooked ham, diced	250 gr
1 cup	2% milk	250 ml
1 cup	Swiss cheese, shredded	250 ml
1/2cup	cottage cheese	125 ml
1/4cup	parmesan cheese +2 Tbsp.	50 ml+ 30 ml
1/4 tsp.	pepper	1 ml
1/4 tsp.	ground nutmeg	1 ml
5	eggs, beaten	
3	egg whites, beaten	

1. Break noodles in half and cook in boiling salted water until done, about 10 minutes. Drain and set aside.

2. In a non-stick skillet, cook ham in a tiny bit of oil for 5 minutes. Combine remaining ingredients in a bowl and then add the ham and fettucine. Mix well.

3. Spoon into a greased 2 quart (2 L) casserole.

4. Cover with top or aluminum foil and chill for 8 hours or overnight. Bake covered at 350F (180C) for 45 minutes. Let stand covered with foil for at least 15 minutes before serving. Serves 6

PASTA WITH BACON,CHEESE AND TOMATO SAUCE

This rich, slightly smoky sauce is cooked for only ten minutes and is satisfyingly good! The longest part is cooking the pasta! Whip out the red and white checkered tablecloth, some Chianti and candles. Serves 4-6

6	bacon slices, chopped or pancetta	
6	garlic cloves, large, finely chopped	
1/2cup	dry red wine (or chicken broth in a pinch)	
28oz.	diced tomatoes in juice (can)	818 ml
1 Tbsp.	tomato paste	15 ml
11/2 tsp.	oregano, dried	7 ml
1/4tsp.	dried crushed red pepper	1 m
4 Tbsp.	Italian parsley or regular, fresh, chopped	60 ml
1 lb.	penne or whatever pasta you prefer	
½ to3/4	cup crumbled blue cheese, feta cheese or coarsely grated Parmesan cheese	

1. Saute bacon in heavy large saucepan over medium heat until crisp. Spoon off all but 4 Tbsp. drippings from pan.

2. Add garlic to pan and stir 30 seconds. Add wine and scrape up any browned bits. Add tomatoes with juices, tomato paste, oregano and crushed red pepper.

3. Simmer until sauce thickens slightly, stirring occasionally, about 10 minutes. Mix in 2 Tbsp parsley.

4. Meanwhile, cook pasta in large pot of boiling salted water until just tender but still firm to bite. Drain, reserving 1/2cup(175ml) cooking water.

5. Return pasta to pot. Add sauce. Toss over heat until sauce coats pasta, adding a little reserved cooking water if mixture is dry. Mix in cheese. Salt and pepper. Top with parsley!

PASTA IN TOMATO CREAM SAUCE WITH SAUSAGE

You could open your own Italian restaurant with this and only have this on the menu. It is rich and has great flavor for minimal effort. Even kids like it. (Use a milder sausage)You can make this sauce a day or so ahead and reheat it at the last minute

1 Tbsp.	butter	15 ml
1 Tbsp.	olive oil	15 ml
1	onion, medium, thinly sliced	
4	garlic cloves, minced	
3/4 lb.	sweet Italian sausage, casings removed	375 gr
2/3 cup	dry white wine	150 ml
28oz.	tomatoes, canned diced peeled with juices	796 ml
1 cup	whipping cream , blend or evaporated skim milk	250ml
6 Tbsp	parsley, fresh, chopped	90 ml
1 lb.	pasta (penne best)	500gr
1 cup	Parmesan cheese, freshly grated.	500gr

1. Melt butter with oil in heavy large skillet over medium-high heat. Add onion and garlic and fry gently until golden brown and tender, about 7 minutes.

2. Add sausage and fry until golden brown and cooked through, breaking up with back of spoon, about 7 minutes. Drain any excess drippings from skillet.

3. Add wine to skillet and boil until almost all liquid evaporates, about 2 minutes. Continued on next page

4 Add tomatoes with juices and simmer 3 minutes. Add cream and simmer until sauce thickens slightly, about 5 minutes. Stir in 4 Tbsp. (60 ml) parsley. Season to taste with salt and pepper.

5. Remove from heat. (Sauce can be prepared 1 day ahead. Cover and refrigerate.)

6. Cook pasta in large pot of boiling salted water until tender but still firm to bite. Drain pasta; transfer to large bowl.

7 .Bring sauce to simmer. Pour sauce over pasta. Add 3/4cup (75ml) cheese and toss to coat. Sprinkle with remaining 1/4 cup (50ml) cheese and 2 tablespoons (30ml) parsley.

You can alter the heat of the dish according to the sausage you use. I prefer a mild sausage. This dish is awesome using the cream but more prudent individuals might use something a little less decadent.

Serves 6.

CHICKEN TETRAZZINI

Peggy Leighton - This is one of Peggy's family favorites. It was passed down to her from her mom and will no doubt be passed on again and again. This is comfort food at its best. Make two and freeze the second for a handy supper. Can also be made ahead and reheated. Great for a potluck table.

8 oz..	spaghetti, broken into 2"(1cm) pieces (2 cups dry)	
1 can	mushrooms, sliced, small can	
4 Tbsp	butter 60 ml	
3 Tbsp.	onion, chopped (1large)	
2 tsp.	celery salt	10 ml
1/8 tsp.	cayenne pepper	1/2 ml
2 tsp.	marjoram	10 ml
2 cans	cream of chicken soup (10oz)	284 ml
1 lg.	can evaporated milk	
2 Tbsp	pimento, chopped	60 ml
3 cups	cooked chicken, cubed	750 ml
2 cups	sharp cheddar cheese, shredded	500 ml
1/4cup	Parmesan cheese	50 ml

1. Cook spaghetti until tender in 1 1/2 quarts (3L)of boiling water. Drain and rinse with hot water

2. Drain mushrooms, saving the liquid.

3. In a medium saucepan, melt the butter and fry the onion until soft.

4. Add the seasonings and mushroom liquid.

5. Blend in the cream of chicken soup and stir until smooth.

6. Gradually add the evaporated milk, stirring constantly until smooth and thickened. Continued on next page

7. In buttered casserole, mix the spaghetti, mushrooms, pimento and chicken. You can divide it between two smaller casserole dishes and freeze one for later.

8. Pour the sauce over and mix well. Top with the cheeses and bake at 350F(180C) for about 30 minutes or until hot and bubbling. Serves 8-10

ELSIE'S CHICKEN CASSEROLE

This recipe belonged to a dear friend of my mothers and was one of her favorite potluck dishes. It has a rich taste and gravy Serve with rice or buttered noodles.

2-3cups	chicken, cooked	500-750 ml
1 can	cream of mushroom soup (undiluted)	284 ml
1 can	Chinese noodles (dry crispy kind)	
1-2	onions, chopped	
1 cup	mushrooms, sliced	250 ml
2 Tbsp.	butter	30 ml
2 cups	chicken broth	500 ml
dash	curry powder	

1 Fry onion in butter until golden, add mushrooms and cook for another five minutes.

3. Pour into a casserole dish, add soup and stir.

4. Add the chicken, chicken broth, dash of curry powder and half of the noodles and stir. Sprinkle the rest of noodles on top

6. Bake at 325F (180C) for 1 hour.

PASTA WITH ARTICHOKES, TOMATOES, PINE NUTS AND BASIL

Lots of pungent ingredients in this pasta dish! It sure gets those taste buds dancing. Very fresh tasting. Some red wine and crusty bread make this a yummy supper.

1/4cup	olive oil	50 ml
1/2cup	pine nuts	125 ml
4	garlic cloves, minced	
2	tomatoes, large, seeded and chopped	
12 oz	marinated artichoke hearts, drained	300 ml
1/4cup	basil, fresh, chopped	50 ml
2 tsp	oregano, fresh, chopped or ½ tsp.(50ml) dried	30 ml
	salt and pepper	
1 lb	angel hair pasta, freshly cooked	500 gr
	black olives, capers	
	grated Parmesan and crumbled feta	

1. Heat oil in heavy medium skillet over medium-high heat. Add pine nuts and fry briefly, add garlic and fry until light brown, (careful, don't burn) about 2 minutes.

2. Stir in tomatoes, artichokes, basil, oregano and (olives or/ and capers if using) and heat through.

3. Season with salt and pepper. Pour over pasta and toss thoroughly. Sprinkle with Parmesan and feta. Serve immediately, passing additional Parmesan separately.

Serves 4.

SIMPLE CURRIED CHICKEN

Mary Lynass - A fragrant, satisfying curry, this dish is very easy to prepare .It has a lovely sauce and is best served with Basmati rice.

1	apple, peeled and chopped	
1	onion, medium, chopped	
1 Tbsp.	butter	15 ml
2 tsp.	ginger powder or 1Tbsp minced fresh ginger	10 ml
2 tsp.	cinnamon	10 ml
2 Tbsp.	flour	30 ml
2 Tbsp.	curry powder	30 ml
2 Tbsp	tomato paste	30 ml
2 tsp.	sugar	10 ml
1-2 cups	chicken, cooked and cut into small pieces	250-500 ml
1/4 cup	raisins (optional)	50 ml
	water	

1. In a large skillet, fry apple and onion (and raisins if using) until soft and golden.

2. Add ginger, cinnamon, curry powder and flour. Fry all for 1 minute.

3. Add tomato paste and sugar. Stir.

4. Add 2 1/2 - 3 cups (500-750ml) of water, stirring to mix until desired thickness. It should be the consistency of gravy.

5. Add the cooked cut up chicken. Simmer over low heat for 10 to 20 minutes, stirring occasionally. If it gets too thick, add a bit of water.

6. Serve with rice and pita bread. Some chutney on the side!

SPEEDY PARMESAN CHICKEN

This is an extremely quick dish to prepare. It is tender and juicy. If you want to be decadent, you can spread the chicken with mayonnaise and coat with mixture or be virtuous and use low fat yoghurt. All variations taste great! Enjoy.

6	chicken breast halves, boneless,skinless (2 lb)	1kg
2 Tbsp	butter, melted	30 ml
1/2 cup	parmesan cheese, grated (2oz)	125 ml
1/4cup	dry bread crumbs	50 ml
1 tsp	dried oregano or basil	5 ml
1 tsp.	dried parsley flakes	5ml
1/4 tsp	paprika,	1 ml
	salt and black pepper	

1. Heat oven to 400 F(200C)

2. Spray 15x10x1-inch baking pan with no stick cooking spray.

3 Dip chicken in butter; coat with combined remaining ingredients.

4. Place in prepared pan. Bake 20 to 25 minutes or until tender.

5. Makes 6 servings.

6. Want it hot and spicy? Substitute 1/4 teaspoon ground red pepper for the black pepper.

This is lovely with a slice of lemon to squeeze over it. Rice and steamed mixed veggies round it out nicely.

LYNN'S BROCCOLI CHICKEN

Lynn Rockwell - This can be made ahead and kept in the fridge overnight and cooked the next day. A great meal if you have a busy day planned, yet want something tasty for supper. It is filling and very satisfying.

2 cups	chicken, cooked, cut into bite sized pieces		500 ml
1 cup	broccoli, flowerettes, cooked		250 ml
2 cups	rice, cooked		500 ml
1 cup	mayonnaise		250 ml
1 can	cream of chicken soup	(10oz)	284 ml
1/2cup	milk		125 ml
1 tsp.	lemon juice		
1 Tbsp.	curry powder		22 ml
2 cups	old cheddar cheese, grated		500 ml

1. Preheat oven to 350F (180C)

2. Mix everything except cheese together and put in a casserole dish. Add some extra milk if too dry.

3. Top with the grated cheese.

4. Bake covered for 40 minutes and uncovered for another 10.

5. Serve with steamed carrots and fresh peas.

RUSSIAN CHICKEN

Venetia Hacquebard - The first time I tasted this I thought I'd died and gone to heaven. Once you have these ingredients on hand you will never be at a loss for what to do with chicken. Easy, very easy to make. Your company will think you've worked for hours preparing this! You can make this a day ahead and bake before serving

8   chicken breasts, skinned and some legs if desired
1 tin   whole cranberries sauce,   340 ml
1 bottle Russian salad dressing (Kraft)(8oz)
1 pkg.   dry onion soup mix or half a pack if you want to cut down on the salt a bit.

1. Preheat oven to 350F(180C)

2. Place chicken in an attractive baking dish. You can use boneless or boned.

3. Mix the rest of the ingredients together and pour over chicken.

4. Bake uncovered for 1 hour. Add a bit of water if mixture dries out. Sauce should be slightly thick.

5. Serve with rice.

SAUCY BLACK SOYA CHICKEN

Tom Duffett - This one of Tom's favorite dishes. Soya sauce turns the chicken really dark. It is quite salty so use low sodium soya sauce if you can and unsalted butter. The drumsticks are terrific for a party. Something different.

1/2cup	soya sauce	125 ml
1 tsp.	crushed chili peppers	5 ml
2 tsp.	pepper	10 ml
3 Tbsp.	lemon juice	45 ml
1 1/2 cups	butter (!!!!) Yes, I put those exclamation marks there. Not for the faint of heart. It originally called for 2 cups of butter.	375 ml
1/3 cup	water	75 ml
3 lbs.	skinned chicken breasts (6 approx.)	
	drumsticks	1.5kg

1. Combine all ingredients in a bowl except chicken and microwave 3 minutes on high to melt butter. Stir to mix.

2. Place chicken breast side down in a baking dish. Pour sauce over.

3. Bake at 400F (200C) for 45-55 minutes basting occasionally and turning chicken once.

4. You can use less chicken but keep the sauce amounts the same. It is great on rice or mashed potatoes.

CHICKEN LAURENTIDE

I've had this recipe since I was nineteen ! It is still a favorite of mine and now my family loves it. A sweet and sour chicken dish. It is better the next day and is wonderful with mashed potatoes to sop up the juice.

6	chicken pieces, skinned thighs or legs	
	seasoned flour, for dredging	
2 cans	crushed tomatoes (28 oz can)	1600 ml
3 Tbsp.	brown sugar	45 ml
1/3 cup.	vinegar	75 ml
1/3 cup	Worcestershire sauce	75 ml
1 Tbsp.	chili powder	15 ml
1 Tbsp.	dry mustard	15 ml
8	garlic cloves, or more!	
	Dash of Tabasco if desired.	

1. Dredge chicken in flour. In a large frying pan, brown in oil or butter on both sides over medium heat.

2. Combine the chicken with the rest of the ingredients in a large pot and simmer for one hour and 15 minutes.

3. Serve over rice or mashed potatoes. This recipe doubles really nicely.

CURRIED HONEY CHICKEN

You would be hard pressed to find an easier recipe for something so yummy! This is a quick to disappear dish at any gathering having the good fortune to serve it.

2 Tbsp.	butter	30 ml
6 Tbsp.	honey	90 ml
2 Tbsp	curry powder	30 ml
1 Tbsp.	mustard	15 ml
1	chicken, cut into pieces. (You could also use drumsticks)	

1. In a pot, melt butter, add honey, curry and mustard.

2. Put chicken in baking dish and pour sauce over chicken.

3. Bake at 350F(180C) for 1 hour (20 minutes in microwave)

QUICK CURRIED CHICKEN OR TURKEY

Peggy Leighton - Another "make in a flash" version of curried chicken. It is delicious served with tiny dishes of all kinds of condiments surrounding it. Try it!

1can	cream of chicken soup (10oz)	284 ml
6 oz.	evaporated milk	200 ml
1/2 cup	chicken broth	125 ml
2 tsp.	curry powder	10 ml
1/2 tsp.	ground ginger	3 ml
1 can	mushrooms, small	
1/2 cup	coconut, shredded	125 ml
2 cups	cooked chicken or turkey pieces	500 ml

1. Heat all together in a double boiler until hot.

2. Serve with rice, Chinese noodles, peanuts, pickled peaches, coconut, Indian chutney (Major Grey), pickled melons, and shredded coconut, raisins etc.

BEEF NACHO CASSEROLE

Carolyn Bourque- Carolyn makes this often on a Saturday night. Her kids love it. Make it in advance, refrigerate and reheat when ready to serve.

1 lb.	ground beef	500 gr
1 1/2 cups	salsa, chunky	375 ml
1 cup	corn, frozen (thawed and drained) or tinned	250 ml
3/4cup	mayonnaise (or sour cream)	175 ml
1 Tbsp.	chili powder	15 ml
2 cups	nacho chips, crushed	500 ml
2 cups	cheese, grated (cheddar or monterey jack)	500ml
	lettuce, shredded	
	tomatoes, chopped	

1. Heat oven to 350F (180C).

2. Brown the beef in a frying pan and drain.

3. Stir in the corn, salsa, chili powder and mayonnaise.

4. In a 2 quart (2L) casserole layer half of the meat mixture, half of the chips and half of the cheese.

5. Repeat the layers.

6. Bake for 20 minutes or until heated. Top with shredded lettuce, chopped tomatoes, and or black olives if desired. Serves 6.

CHEESEBURGER PIE

Excellent! The topping simple as it is, gives this pie its distinctive flavour. I often make this pie for a weekend supper. It is good reheated too, so you can make it a day ahead. Serve with dill pickles, salad and rolls.

1	9" unbaked pie shell	
1 lb.	ground beef, lean or extra lean	500 gr
1/2 cups	evaporated skim milk	500 ml
1/3 cup	breadcrumbs	75 ml
1/2 cups	onion, chopped	500 ml
3/4 tsp	salt	3 ml
1 tsp.	oregano	5 ml
1/8 tsp.	pepper (dash)	
11/2 cups	cheddar cheese, grated	375 ml
3 tsp.	Worcestershire sauce	15 ml

1. Preheat oven to 350F (180C)

2. Combine the meat and all ingredients except cheese and Worcestershire sauce.

3. Pat into the unbaked pastry shell. and bake for 35- 40 minutes.

4. Toss cheese with Worcestershire sauce and spread on top of meat mixture and bake 10 minutes more.

5. Serves approximately 6.

BOBOTIE

Venetia Hacquebard - This is a classic dish from South Africa's Cape Town. A very different, delicious dish to present to your eating companions. It is made with ground beef and feeds a crowd. Savory, with a hint of sweet and a touch of curry. Serve with rice and lots of condiments!

1/2 cup	sultana raisins, firmly packed	125 ml
1"	ginger, fresh, peeled and minced	2cm
2	onions, chopped (1/2 lb.)	250 gr
2 Tbsp.	oil	30 ml
2 lb.	ground beef	500 gr
2 1/2 Tbsp.	curry powder, or more to taste	38 ml
1 cup	mango chutney	250 ml
1/2 cup	almonds, slivered	125 ml
2 Tbsp.	cider vinegar, or more to taste	30 ml
2 Tbsp.	turmeric	30 ml
5	eggs	
4	bay leaves	
1 1/2 cups	half and half cream	375 ml

1. Fry the onion and ginger over low heat until soft. (5 minutes)

2. Add beef and stir and cook until no pink remains.(8 minutes)

3. Sprinkle the curry powder over the top and salt and pepper.

4. Coarsely chop the chutney and stir into the beef mixture with the vinegar, almonds, raisins and turmeric. Adjust seasoning, adding more vinegar, salt, curry etc. (Can cool completely and refrigerate for up to two days at this point.)

5. Heat oven to 350 F(180C). Beat 1 egg and mix it thoroughly with the beef and transfer the mixture to a deep 2 1/2 quart (2L) casserole or 9 x 13 (3.5L)dish. Continued next page

6. Insert the bay leaves upright into the casserole. Mix the eggs with the cream and pour over meat.

7. Bake 40-50 minutes until custard is set and lightly glazed. Remove bay leaves. Can keep casserole warm in oven 200 F for 30-40 minutes.

8. Serve with rice and side dishes of peanuts, coconut, chutney etc.

BUSY WOMAN'S BEEF BOURGUIGNONNE

This has got to be one of the all time best recipes for the least effort I know. It is so flavourful!! Makes a rich gravy. Comfort food at its best.

3 lbs.	stewing beef	1.5 kg
1 cup	sliced mushrooms	250 ml
1 pkg.	dry onion soup mix	
1 pkg.	mushroom soup mix	
11/2 cups	apple juice	375 ml
1 cup	burgundy red wine	250 ml

1. Place all ingredients in a slow cooker and mix well.

2. Cook on low setting for 10 hours.

3. Serve over hot buttered noodles with a salad, some crusty bread and a glass of red wine.

4. Can be slowly cooked, covered in the oven at 325 (180C) for 3 hours. Check to make sure liquid doesn't evaporate. Add water if needed.

EASY CABBAGE ROLL CASSEROLE

I love cabbage rolls but they take so long to make. This is just as delicious and is made in a snap. If you are really in a hurry, substitute spaghetti sauce for the tomatoes and paste. The cinnamon and mint give it a Middle Eastern flavor and can be omitted if you would like a less exotic taste.

1 lb	ground beef	500 gr.
3	cloves of garlic, minced (3tsp)	15 ml
2	onions, medium, chopped	
1 cup	rice, uncooked	250 ml
28 oz	tomatoes, canned, chopped	796 ml
2 Tbsp.	tomato paste	30 ml
1/2 cup	chicken stock or water	125 ml
6 cups	cabbage, shredded (1.5) or 2 packages of ready made coleslaw (8oz.each)	1.5L
2 Tbsp.	cinnamon	30 ml
1 tsp	mint	15 ml
	salt and pepper to taste	

1. In a large frying pan, cook the beef and onions and garlic until there is no pink left in the beef. Add salt and pepper.

2. Add the uncooked rice to the beef mixture and set aside.

3. Mix together the tomatoes, tomato paste, water, cinnamon and mint

4. In a large casserole dish, 3 qt. (1.5 L), layer half of the cabbage. Cover with half of the beef mixture. Cover that with half of the sauce.

5. Put in the rest of the cabbage, then the beef and top with the rest of the sauce.

6. Cover and bake at 350F (180C) for 1 - 1 1/2hours without stirring. Stand for 10 minutes before serving. Serves 6

HAWAIIAN SAUSAGE CASSEROLE

Everyone in our family loves this colorful meal. Dig out the flowered shirts! Serve over rice.

1 1/2 lb.	sausage (we like the honey/garlic kind)	750gr
1/2	green pepper, chopped	
1/2	red pepper, chopped	
2	celery stalks, chopped	
1	onion, chopped	
20 oz.	pineapple chunks (canned), save juice	540 ml
1/4 cup	vinegar	50 ml
1 1/2Tbsp	soya sauce	22ml
2 Tbsp	cornstarch	30 ml
1/4 cup	brown sugar	50 ml
1 Tbsp.	olive oil	15 ml

1. Fry the sausage for 20 minutes or so, until cooked and cut into bite sized slices. Drain fat and set aside.

2. In the same frying pan, add the oil and fry the peppers, onion and celery until softened. Add the pineapple chunks.

3. Mix together the sugar and cornstarch. Combine the pineapple juice, vinegar and soya sauce and stir into the sugar mixture.

4.. Slowly add the liquid mixture to the veggie mixture, stirring until thickened. Taste and add more soya, sugar or vinegar to your liking.

5. Add the sausages and gently heat them. Serve over a bed of rice.

6. If serving later, pour sausage mixture into a covered casserole dish, refrigerate and reheat before serving

HANIA'S COMFORT STEW

Hania Kacszkowski – A hearty, healthy meal that makes terrific leftovers! This is high in fibre and low in fat.

6	sun-dried tomato sausages	
28 oz	tomatoes with spices, canned	796 ml
1 can	white beans(19 oz)	540 ml
1 can	Italian (Romano) beans (19oz)	540 ml
2	onions, chopped	
2	carrots, large, sliced	
1	stalk celery, chopped (optional)	
3 cups	brown rice, cooked	750 ml
1/2tsp	basil	2 ml
1/2tsp	oregano	2 ml
1 tsp	cumin seeds	5 ml
	salt and pepper to taste	

1. Cook onions and carrots (and celery if using) in 1/3 cups of water in a large covered pot for about 5 minutes. Add the beans and the tomatoes and spices.

2. Meanwhile, cut the sausages into bite sized pieces. Put into a medium pot with water and boil until cooked through. Most of the fat will boil out but none of the flavor.

3. Add the sausages to the pot with the vegetables.

4. Add the brown rice. Stir and heat on medium low until heated throughout. Serves 6 generously. Bon Appetit!

EASY GLAZED MEATLOAF

This has been a family standard for years. It has a sweet tangy tomato topping. Terrific with mashed potatoes and peas. Real comfort food.

2	eggs, beaten	
3/4cup	milk	75 ml
2/3 cup	bread crumbs	150 ml
1	onion, minced	
1 tsp.	salt	5 ml
1/2 tsp.	oregano	3 ml
11/2 lb.	ground beef	750 gr
	pepper, dash	
1/4cup	ketchup	50 ml
2 Tbsp.	brown sugar	30 ml
1 tsp.	dry mustard	5 ml
1/2 tsp.	nutmeg	3 ml

1. In a big bowl, mix together the eggs, milk, crumbs, onion, salt, pepper and oregano.

2. Add the ground beef and mix well. Pat the mixture into a loaf pan.

3. Bake at 350F (180C) for 1 hour.

4. Combine the remaining ingredients and spread on top of meatloaf.

5. Bake another 15 minutes.

6. Serves 6

DECEMBER TOURTIERE

This is a traditional meat pie recipe that originates in Quebec. Full of aromatic spices, it is good hot or cold. Easy to make and terrific served with cranberry relish on the side.

11/2 lb	ground beef	750 gr
11/2 lb	ground pork	750 gr
2	onions, chopped	
1 tsp.	salt	5 ml
11/2 tsp	thyme	7ml
11/2 tsp	dry mustard	7ml
11/2 tsp	sage	7ml
1 tsp	cloves	5 ml
1/2 tsp	cinnamon	3 ml
3	garlic cloves, minced	
1 cup	mashed potato water	250 ml
2	potatoes, medium, cooked and mashed	500 ml
2	pie shells, uncooked	

1. Mix all ingredients in large saucepan except for potatoes Bring to boiling point and cook uncovered for 30 minutes.

2. Add mashed potato and mix well. Cool and fill the 2 pie shells. Bake at 425F(220C) for 30 minutes or until shell is cooked.

QUICK AND EASY ASIAN BEEF AND NOODLES

Fastest dish in the East! Take advantage of some packaged coleslaw mix and ramen soup. Good too. Something different to take to a potluck.

2	rib-eye steaks (8 oz. each)	500 gr
2 tsp.	dark Sesame oil, divided	10 ml
2 cups	green onions, sliced into 1" lengths	500 ml
4 cups	coleslaw mix, prepackaged	1 L
3 pkgs.	beef-flavour ramen noodle soup(2.8oz.) MINUS two seasoning packages	
3 cups	water	750 ml
1-2 Tbsp.	soy sauce (low sodium)	15 -30 ml

1. Trim the fat from the steak and cut across the grain diagonally into thin slices. Heat 1 tsp. of oil in a large non-stick frying pan and add steak and onions.

2. Fry 1 minute, stirring. Remove mixture from pan. Heat the rest of the oil in the pan and add the coleslaw, stirring for 30 seconds or so, until slightly softened. Remove from pan and add to steak mixture.

3. Take noodles out of packages and *discard* 2 of the seasoning packs. Add the 3 cups of water and the seasoning packs to the frying pan and bring to a boil.

4. Break the noodles in half and add to the water. Cook 2 minutes or until most of the liquid is absorbed, stirring often.

5. Stir in the steak mixture and soy sauce and heat through. This makes about 4 cups.

OVEN BARBEQUED ORIENTAL PORK TENDERLOINS

Carolyn Bourque – Yowza these are good!

2 Tbsp.	soy sauce, light	30 ml
2 Tbsp.	hoisin sauce	30 ml
1 Tbsp.	sherry	15 ml
1 Tbsp.	black bean sauce	
11/2 tsp.	gingerroot, minced	7 ml
11/2tsp.	brown sugar, packed	7 ml
1	garlic clove, minced	
2 tsp.	sesame oil	10 ml
pinch	5-Spice Powder *	
2 lbs.	pork tenderloins (2X3/4 lb each approx.)	1 kg

1. Mix together all the marinade ingredients in a bowl.

2. Place the tenderloins in a shallow glass baking dish and cover with marinade coating all sides. Marinate pork for several hours(up to 8) covered, in fridge, turning occasionally.

3 Bake at 375F (190C) for 30-35 minutes. Brush with marinade halfway through. Tent with foil and let stand 5 minutes before slicing. Slice thin to serve.

4. Tenderloin is cooked when thermometer inserted into center registers 165F.(74C)

   * available in Oriental section of grocery store.

SHRIMP WITH FETA

A fragrant and relatively low fat meal. Serve with crusty French bread and a glass of wine.

2 lb.	shrimp	1 kg
4 Tbsp.	olive oil	60 ml
1/2 cup	onions, chopped	125 ml
2	cloves garlic	
5	tomatoes, skinned and seeded and chopped	
1/2cup	white wine	125 ml
1/2 tsp.	oregano	2 ml
1/2	basil	2 ml
2 Tbsp.	parsley	30 ml
	ground pepper	
5 oz	feta cheese, crumbled	165 ml

1. In shallow pan, fry onion with garlic until soft.

2. Add the tomatoes, wine, herbs, and dash of pepper. Cook until sauce thickens slightly.

3. Add the shrimp and cook gently, about 5 minutes.

4. Now add the feta cheese and sprinkle with some extra parsley if you would like. Serves 4

SOUR CREAM SHRIMP

This is soooo good. Use non-fat sour cream to lighten the load a bit.

2 lb.	shrimp, peeled, deveined	1 kg
5 Tbsp.	butter (1/3 cup)	75 ml
6 Tbsp.	mushrooms, sliced	90 ml
1/2 cups	sour cream	500 ml
2 tsp.	soy sauce	10 ml
1/2 cups	Parmesan cheese, grated	500 ml
	salt, pepper, paprika to taste	

1. In a frying pan, melt the butter and fry the shrimp for about 2 minutes. Add the mushrooms and cook for another 3 minutes.

2. In a saucepan, heat the sour cream just until it starts to simmer and reduce heat. Add the soy sauce, salt and pepper and just enough paprika to turn the sauce pink.

3. Cook over low heat until slightly thickened and add shrimp and mushrooms. Pour into shallow casserole dish and top with Parmesan cheese.

4. Broil until cheese is melted and bubbling.

5. Serve with rice.

CAJUN SHRIMP

These are certainly zippy! Really delicious flavour but quite spicy so use less hot sauce for a more civilized dish. A real Cajun treat.

6-9	slices bacon	
	oil	
1/4 cup	hot sauce	50 ml
2 Tbsp.	Dijon mustard	30 ml
1 tsp.	oregano	5 ml
1 tsp.	chili powder	5 ml
1/2 tsp.	basil	3 ml
1/2 tsp.	thyme	3 ml
1/2 tsp.	ground black pepper	1 ml
3-4	cloves garlic, minced	
1 lb	shrimp, large, uncooked, shelled, deveined	500 gr

1. In large frying pan, cook bacon until crisp. Pour the drippings into a glass measuring cup and add oil to make 1/3 cup(75ml)

2. Pour the drippings back into the pan and add the rest of the ingredients and cook for 5-7 minutes or until the shrimp is cooked.

3. Spoon the shrimp mixture over a mound of rice to serve.

SALMON STEAKS IN MUSTARD SAUCE

The zippy sauce really complements the salmon well. I really like the grainy Dijon mustard but you have to use a wee bit more.

4	salmon steaks	
2 Tbsp.	Dijon mustard	30 ml
1 Tbsp.	lemon juice	15 ml
1 Tbsp.	butter, melted	15 ml
	salt and pepper	
1 Tbsp	shallots or onion, finely minced	15 ml
	tin foil	

1. Tear off a large piece of tin foil and place in the bottom of a baking dish. Put the salmon steaks on top of the foil.

2. Combine the rest of the ingredients and spread over the top of the steaks. Fold the foil over and seal securely.

3. Bake at 425F (220C) for 20 – 40 minutes depending on thickness of steaks. 10 minutes per 1 inch (2cm) thickness of steak. Do not check until after 15 minutes have passed.

THAI SALMON STEAKS

This sauce can be used with chicken also!

4-6	salmon steaks	
1/4 cup	butter	50 ml
1	garlic clove, minced	
2 Tbsp.	ginger, fresh minced	30 ml
1/4cup	lime juice	50 ml
1 Tbsp.	soya sauce	15 ml
1 tsp.	Dijon mustard	5 ml
1 tsp.	sesame oil or peanut oil	5 ml
1 Tbsp	brown sugar	15 ml

1. Gently fry the ginger and garlic in the butter.

2. Add the lime juice, soya sauce, mustard, oil and brown
   sugar. Simmer a few minutes.(2-3)

3. Pour the sauce over the salmon in a baking dish. Cover with
   tin foil and bake at 425F (220C) for 10 -12 minutes per inch
   (2cm) of thickest part of fish.

MIGAS BARBEQUED SALMON OR TROUT

Anna Migas - If the pot luck includes a BBQ, then take some fish along with this sauce and copies of the recipe because everyone will want to know how you made it.....

1 fillet   salmon or trout, skin on
              Lowry's Lemon Pepper
              salt
              mayonnaise (not salad dressing)
              lemon juice

1. Season the fish fillet with generous amounts of Lowry's lemon pepper and salt,

2. In a 4 to 1 ration, mix together the mayonnaise and lemon juice. (example: 1 cup (250 ml) mayo to 1/4cup(50 ml) lemon)

3. Cook the fish, skin side down on BBQ and dab on mayo mixture

4. The meat next to skin will turn pale when done. Then cut fish into 1 person portions/ segments and carefully flip it over back onto the skin. No further seasoning.

5. Says Anna, this has been our family summer favorite for years at BBQ get togethers.

CHRISTMAS EVE SEAFOOD CASSEROLE

Carolyn Bourque- This is a really special casserole. Not one you make very often but a show stopper when you do!

3 Tbsp.	butter	45 ml
1cup	onion, finely chopped	250 ml
1/2 cup	mushrooms, finely chopped	175 ml
1/2 cup	celery, finely chopped	175 ml
1	garlic clove, pressed	
2 lb.	scallops	1 kg
1/4cup	sherry	50 ml
1 tsp.	lemon juice	5 ml
11oz	lobster meat, thawed	286 gr
1 can	baby clams, drained	
11oz.	crab meat, thawed and drained	286 gr
2 lb.	shrimp, thawed and drained	1 kg
1/2cup	butter	125 ml
1/4cup	flour	50 ml
2 cups	cream, 35%	500 ml
1 Tbsp.	Dijon mustard	15 ml
dash	Worcestershire sauce, Cayenne pepper, and salt	
1 Tbsp.	fresh parsley, chopped	15 ml
2cups	old cheddar cheese, grated	500 ml
11/4cup	croutons	300 ml

1. In a medium saucepan, fry the onion, mushrooms and celery in 3 Tbsp. butter until soft.

2. Add garlic and scallops, increase heat to medium and cook until scallops are no longer translucent (aprox. 1 minute)

3. Stir in sherry and transfer mixture to a glass or steel bowl. Add lemon juice. Continued on next page

4. To the mixture in the bowl, add lobster, clams, crab and shrimp. Toss gently and set aside.

5. Meanwhile, in a saucepan over medium heat, melt 1/2cup of butter. Slowly add the flour, whisking constantly until the flour is lump free and is cooked (aprox. 2 minutes).

6. Slowly whisk in cream. Add Worcestershire sauce, Dijon, cayenne. Bring to a soft boil, whisking constantly and stir in 1 cup of the cheddar cheese.

7. Add this to the seafood mixture and mix together. Add the parsley.

8. Transfer to a buttered baking dish and top with croutons and 1 cup grated cheese.

9. Bake at 375F(190C) for 20 minutes or until bubbly and golden. Brown under preheated broiler.

10. Serves 6-8. Great with rice and salad.

HADDOCK CASSEROLE

Dot Lavers - This can also be made with just scallops. A mild tasting casserole that goes well with everything. Serve with rice.

2 lb.	haddock fillets or 1 lb scallops (500gr)	1 kg
2-3	hard-boiled eggs	
3Tbsp.	butter	45 ml
3Tbsp.	flour	45 ml
13/4 cup	milk	425 ml
1 tsp .	lemon juice	5 ml
	salt and pepper	
	breadcrumbs	
2 cups	cheddar cheese, grated	500 ml

1. In saucepan, melt butter and add flour, stirring constantly.

2. Cook for 2 minutes. Add milk, lemon juice and salt and pepper.

3. Stir until thickened and smooth. Take off heat.

4. Put fish in casserole dish and scatter cut up hard-boiled eggs around the top.

5. Pour sauce over all.

6. Sprinkle with breadcrumbs and dot with butter. Sprinkle cheese on top.

7. Bake 25 -30 minutes at 350F (180C).

NANCY'S SEAFOOD CASSEROLE

Nancy Conn- Nancy serves this when she wants a special dish for company. It is delicious and very rich and people usually go home with the recipe. Can be made ahead and reheated before serving.

2 cups	chopped celery	500 ml
2 cups	chopped onion	500 ml
2 Tbsp.	oil	30 ml
3/4cup	flour	75 ml
3 cups	milk	750 ml
1 lb.	Velveeta cheese	500 gr
½ cup	butter	125 ml
1 lg. tin	lobster	
1 lb.	scallops	500gr
3/4 lb.	shrimp	375 gr
1 1/2lb.	fish fillets (haddock or any white fish)	750 gr

1. In a large pot, fry the onion and celery in oil until soft and golden.

2. Add the butter to the pot and stir until melted.

3. Sprinkle the flour over all and stir until mixed and thick. Slowly add the milk stirring all the while to mix evenly without lumps.

4. Add the Velveeta cheese and stir over low heat until melted.

5. Add the seafood to the sauce and pour the entire mixture into an oven - proof casserole dish.

6. Bake uncovered at 350F(180C) for approximately 30 minutes until bubbly. Serve with rice.

SWEETS

NOVA SCOTIA MILE HIGH BISCUITS

Kathy Greenwood - These are fluffy, melt in your mouth biscuits. Great for strawberry shortcake base. A tip to keep the biscuits all the same size is to put the pan of biscuits in the fridge for a few minutes before baking.

3 cups	flour	750 ml
41/2 tsp	baking powder	22 ml
3/4 tsp	cream of tartar	3 ml
2 1/2Tbsp	sugar	38 ml
3/4 tsp.	salt	3 ml
3/4 cup	shortening	175 ml
1	egg, lightly beaten	
1 cup	milk	250 ml

1. Preheat the oven to 450F (230C) and grease a baking sheet.

2. In a bowl, sift together the dry ingredients.

3. Cut in the shortening till it resembles coarse meal.

4. Mix the milk and the lightly beaten egg together.

5. Add the egg mixture to the dry with a fork.

6. Fork lightly until dough holds together.

7. Turn out dough onto lightly floured board and knead softly with floured fingers.

8. Roll dough 1 inch thick and cut with floured cutter.

9. Arrange apart on sheet and bake for 12 minutes or until done.

TWEED SQUARES

Ella Cameron – One of Cape Breton's best bakers! These are a popular sweet here. You'll find them at baby showers, bridge games, weddings and wakes.

1/2 cup	butter	125 ml
2/3 cup	sugar	150 ml
1 1/3 cup	flour	325 ml
2 tsp.	baking powder	10 ml
1 tsp.	vanilla	5 ml
1/2 cup	milk	250 ml
2	egg whites, beaten	
2	squares semi-sweet chocolate, grated	50 gr
1/3 cup	butter	75 ml
1 1/2 cup	icing sugar	375 ml
2	egg yolks	
2	squares semi-sweet chocolate	50 gr
2 Tbsp.	butter	30 ml

1. Cream 1/2 cup (125ml) butter and sugar together

2. Add flour, baking powder, vanilla, alternately with milk.

3. Fold in beaten egg whites and grated chocolate.

4. Grease a 9 x 9" (2.5L) pan well and pour in mixture. Bake 25 - 30 minutes at 350F (180C). COOL.

5. Beat 1/3 cup butter. Add icing sugar and mix till creamy. Add egg yolks and beat till creamy.

6. Put on cooled squares. Melt together the remaining chocolate and butter and spread over the top of squares.

7. Set in the fridge until the top hardens.

PEANUT BUTTER CHOCOLATE RICE CRISPIE SQUARES (SQUAMISH BARS)

The first time I had these was at our street party and they were gobbled up lickety split They are sort of like a Nanaimo bar but better (in my opinion) Millions would probably disagree but I think they are yummy! They can be frozen for up to a month.

1 cup	peanut butter	250 ml
½ cup	brown sugar	125 ml
½ cup	corn syrup	125 ml
2 cups	rice crispies	250 ml
¼ cup	butter	50 ml
2 cups	icing sugar	500 ml
2 Tbsp	milk	30 ml
1½ tsp	vanilla	7 ml
3oz	semi-sweet chocolate	150 gr
1Tbsp.	butter	15 ml

1. Lightly grease a 9 x 13 (3.5L) dish

2. In a large pot, cook over medium heat until melted, peanut butter, corn syrup and brown sugar. Remove from heat.

3. Stir in the rice crispies until well mixed. Pat into the dish and let cool.

4. In a bowl, mix together the ¼ cup butter, vanilla, icing sugar and milk until well blended. Spread on the cooled rice crispie mixture.

5. Melt together the chocolate and the 1Tbsp. butter. Pour this over the icing mixture on the squares.

6. Cut just after you have finished frosting, it is easier.

MILFORD'S FAVOURITE SQUARES

Dot Lavers- This is a one saucepan special! Use whatever you have on hand.

1/2cup	butter	125 ml
1 cup	brown sugar	250 ml
1	egg	
1 cup	flour	250 ml
1 tsp	baking powder	5 ml
1 tsp	vanilla	5 ml
1/2 tsp	salt	2 ml
1 cup	any combination of nuts, cherries, coconut, dates, chocolate, dried cranberries etc.	250 ml

1. Melt the butter and sugar in a saucepan. Cool.

2. Add the egg and beat in quickly. Add the vanilla, flour, baking powder and salt.

3. Add the coconut/fruit mixture. If you want, you can just add coconut only or fruit only or any combination that tickles your fancy!

4. Press into a square pan and bake at 350F (180C) for 25 minutes.

ENGLISH TOFFEE SQUARES

These are also a snap to make with a chocolate and butterscotch taste. Crunchy,chewy and yummy!.

1 cup	butter	250 ml
1 cup	brown sugar	250 ml
1 tsp.	vanilla	5 ml
2 cups	flour	500 ml
6 oz.	chocolate chips	175 ml
1 cup	pecans	250 ml

1. Grease and flour a 8x8" pan and preheat oven to 350 (180C).

2. Melt butter. Add sugar and vanilla and mix.

3. Add the rest of the ingredients and pat into floured pan.

4. Bake at 350F(180C) for 30 minutes until just done. Be careful not to overcook

5. If desired you could substitute white chocolate chips and almonds.

CHOCOLATE PUDDING CAKE

Joanne Duffett –This makes its own sauce! It is a strange way to make a cake, like a science experiment but it works! Delicious warm with cold ice cream.

1 cup	flour	250 ml
2 tsp	baking powder	10 ml
1/4 tsp	salt	1 ml
1/2 cup	sugar	125 ml
2 Tbsp.	cocoa powder	30 ml
2 Tbsp.	butter, softened	30 ml
1/2cup	milk, warm	125 ml
1/2cup	brown sugar	125 ml
3 Tbsp.	cocoa powder	45 ml
2 1/2 cups boiling water		625 ml

1. In a large bowl, mix together the first five ingredients.

2. Add the butter and warm milk, beat with a wooden spoon.

3. Pour into a greased 8 x 8"" (1L) pan and spread evenly.

4. Mix together the brown sugar and cocoa and sprinkle over the batter. Pour the boiling water overall of it. (Sounds strange but it works)

5. Bake at 350F (180C) for 45-55 minutes

LUSCIOUS LEMON SQUARES

Debra Morris – Light, lemony and easy.

30	graham wafers, crushed (2 1/2 cups)	750 ml
1/2cup	melted butter	125 ml
14 oz	sweetened condensed milk (can)	397 ml
2	lemons squeezed (1/2 cup juice)	125 ml
2	egg yolks	
2	egg whites, beaten till stiff	

1. Combine the graham crumbs and butter. Press into a 8 x 8" pan.

2. In a bowl, combine the sweetened condensed milk, lemon juice, and egg yolks.

3. Fold in the beaten egg whites.

4. Gently spread over the graham crust and sprinkle some crumbs over the top.

5. Bake at 300F (150C) for 10 -15 minutes.

CRANBERRY ALMOND SQUARES

Judy Wensel - These are tender, moist melt in your mouth delicious. More like a cake than a square. The almond flavouring gives them a special touch. These are a huge favourite and they are even better the next day.

1 1/2 cup	sugar	375 ml
2 lg.	eggs	
3/4 cup	unsalted butter, melted ,cooled slightly	75 ml
1 tsp.	almond extract	5 ml
1 1/2 cup	flour	375 ml
2 cups	cranberries, fresh or frozen	500 ml
1/2 cup	almonds or pecans , chopped	125 ml

1. Preheat oven to 350F (180C). Butter a 9" (1L) square pan.

2. In a large bowl using an electric mixer, beat sugar and eggs for 2 minutes.

3. Beat in butter and almond extract.

4. Stir in flour.

5. Stir in berries and nuts.

6. Bake at 350F (180C) for about 1 hour until a stick inserted in it comes out clean.

7. Transfer to a rack and cool completely.

8. Cover tightly and let stand at room temperature.

SEX IN A PAN

It has a silly name and it has been around for awhile, but this dessert is still luscious! It gets raves when ever I serve it. This also freezes well. Just make sure to thaw it out completely in the fridge before serving.

1 cup	pecans or almonds, ground	250 ml
3 Tbsp.	sugar	45 ml
1 cup	flour	250 ml
1/2 - 3/4 cup	butter	125 ml
8 oz	cream cheese, softened	250 gr
35 oz	Cool Whip (do not substitute whipped cream, it won't work)	
1 cup	icing sugar	250 ml
6oz.pkg.	instant vanilla pudding mix	170 ml
6oz.pkg.	instant chocolate pudding mix	170 ml
2 cups	milk	250 ml

1. Mix together, nuts, flour, butter and sugar until crumbly. Pat into a greased 9x13" (3.5L) pan. Bake at 325F (170C) for 25 minutes. Cool.

2. Mix cream cheese, icing sugar and half the Cool Whip, spread over the baked base.

3. Beat the vanilla pudding mix with 1 cup (250 ml) milk for 2-3 minutes and then spread over the Cool Whip layer.

4. Beat chocolate pudding mix with 1 cup (250 ml) milk for 2-3 minutes and spread over vanilla layer.

5. Cover with the remaining Cool Whip and garnish with shaved chocolate. This can be made ahead and frozen.

CARAMEL SHORTBREAD

Hazel McNab- We called these Mars Bars growing up but caramel shortbread says it all. This was my Scottish grandmother's recipe. Everyone loves them.

2 cups	butter or margarine, divided.	500 ml
1/3+1/4 cup	sugar, divided	75 ml / 50 ml
1 cup	flour	250 ml
3 Tbsp.	almonds, ground *	45 ml
2 Tbsp.	corn syrup	30 ml
14oz	sweetened condensed milk	397 ml
12 oz	semisweet choc chips or chocolate squares	
		325 gr
1/4 cup	almonds, sliced *	50 ml

1. Preheat oven to 350F(180C).

2. In a bowl, beat one cup of butter and 1/3cup(75ml) of sugar.

3. Stir in the flour and ground almonds to form a dough.

4. Press the dough into a greased 9 x 13" pan or 8 x 8"

5. Bake for approx. 25 minutes or until crust is pale golden.

6. Meanwhile, in a saucepan over medium heat, melt the butter and sugar, corn syrup and milk. Bring to a boil . Reduce the heat and stir until the mixture thickens.

7 Spread the caramel over the shortbread. Chill.

8. Melt the chocolate chips and spread over the caramel. Top with the almonds. Chill.

**The almonds can be omitted entirely from the recipe if desired. Just add an extra 3 Tbsp. of flour.

CINNAMON SWIRL LOAF

This is a terrific, simple tasty loaf for a snack or breakfast! Easy to make and yummy too. You can add a handful of pecans or walnuts for a bit more oomph!

1/2cup	butter	125 ml
2	eggs	
1 cup	sour cream or yoghurt	250 ml
1 tsp	baking powder	5 ml
2 tsp	vanilla	10 ml
1 cup	white sugar	250 ml
2 cups	flour	500 ml
1/2 tsp	baking soda	2 ml
	dash salt	
3 Tbsp	brown sugar	45 ml
1 Tbsp	cinnamon	15 ml
	dash allspice	

1. Preheat oven to 350F (180C). Grease loaf pan.

2. Beat all ingredients and spread half of the mixture in a loaf pan.

3. Mix together the cinnamon mixture and spread over first layer. (add some pecans if using)

4. Put on remaining cake batter and cut through with a knife, to sort of swirl through the cinnamon. **If you want you can make a bit of extra topping and sprinkle it on top before baking.**

5. Bake at 350F(180C) for 45-50 minutes.

APRICOT HONEY LOAF

This is a non-traditional Jewish New Year cake. Moist and not overly sweet. If you like, you can use cognac instead of rum! You can also serve it with some sweetened whipped cream or ice cream but it is usually served alone as is!

1/2 cup	dried apricots, roughly chopped	125 ml
1/4 cup	dark rum	50 ml
2 large	eggs	
1 cup	clover honey	250 ml
1/3 cup	vegetable oil	75 ml
1	lemon, grated peel and juice	
1	orange, grated peel and juice	
1/3 cup	sugar	75 ml
1 tsp	salt	5 ml
1/3 cup	apricot jam	75 ml
2 cups	unbleached all-purpose flour	500 ml
1/2 tsp	baking soda	2 ml
1/2 cup	slivered almonds or chopped walnuts or cashews	
		125 ml

1. In a small bowl, soak the apricots in the rum for at least 30 minutes.

2. Preheat the oven to 350F(180C) and grease a 10- by 5-inch loaf pan.

3. In a mixing bowl, beat the eggs with a whisk. Stir in the honey, vegetable oil, grated lemon and orange rind and juice, sugar, salt, and apricot jam.

4.Sift the flour and the baking soda into another bowl.

5. Strain the apricots, reserving the excess rum.

Continued on the next page.

6. Add the flour alternately with the rum to the honey mixture. Fold in the apricots.

7. Scoop the batter into the prepared pan and sprinkle with the nuts.

8. Bake in the oven on the lower rack for 50-55 minutes, or until the center of the cake is firm when you press it. Keep an eye on it so it doesn't scorch on the outside. Remove from the oven and cool on a rack.

LEMON POPPY SEED LOAF

Angela Quinn - I got this recipe from Angela one Christmas and it is lovely. I like it super lemony so I usually add a bit more lemon rind and lemon to the glaze.

1/2cup	butter, softened	125 ml
1 cup	sugar	250 ml
2	eggs	
1 tsp.	lemon rind, grated	5 ml
11/2 cup	flour	375 ml
1 tsp.	baking soda	5 ml
1/2 tsp	salt	2 ml
1/3 cup	milk	75 ml
2 Tbsp.	poppy seeds	30 ml
	juice of one big lemon	
1/2 cup	confectioner's sugar	125 ml

1. Heat the oven to 350F (180C). Grease a 9x5 loaf pan (2L)

2. In a large mixing bowl, beat together the butter and sugar. Add the eggs, beating well.

3. Add the dry ingredients alternately with the milk. Add the poppy seeds.

4. Pour the batter into the pan and bake at 350F (180C) for 55 minutes or until a toothpick inserted in the center comes out clean. Let the loaf cool for 15 minutes then unmold it and place on rack with wax paper underneath.

5. Meanwhile mix together the lemon juice and confectioner's sugar. Prick the loaf all over and pour the glaze over the top.

119

ZUCCHINI ALMOND CAKE

Jane Cooley -This is to die for. It is a very moist cake that keeps well for up to 10 days. It has a glazed topping but some swear that a cream cheese frosting topped with toasted almonds is better. You be the judge, try it both ways!

3 cups	flour	750 ml
2 tsp.	baking powder	10 ml
1 tsp.	baking soda	5 ml
1 tsp.	salt	5 ml
4	eggs	
3 cups	sugar	750 ml
1 cup	oil	250 ml
1 tsp.	almond extract	
3 cups	zucchini, finely grated	750 ml
1 cups	almonds, ground	250 ml
11/2 cups	icing sugar	
2 Tbsp.	milk	30 ml
1/4 tsp.	almond extract	1 ml
1/4 cup	toasted sliced almonds	50 ml

1. Grease and flour tube pan and preheat oven to 350F (180C).

2. In bowl, sift together flour, baking powder, soda, and salt.

3. In large bowl, beat eggs until thick and gradually add sugar. Stir in oil and almond extract.

4. Add the dry ingredients ,mix until smooth. Stir in almonds.

5. Bake for 1 hour and 15 minutes or till toothpick comes clean.

6. Spread with almond glaze or cream cheese frosting.

FOR GLAZE: Blend icing sugar, milk, and extract. Pour over cooled cake and top with toasted almonds.

ORANGE SOAKED CAKE

Pam Noseworthy – The first time I had this was on my birthday and it is still one of my favourite cakes. It has a dense buttery texture and the orange soaking makes it really special! Decorate with fresh edible flowers.

1 cup	butter	250 ml
2 cups	sugar	500 ml
4	eggs	
3Tbsp.	orange rind	45 ml
3 cups	flour	750 ml
2 tsp.	baking powder	10 ml
1/2 tsp	salt	
2 ml		
1 cup	milk	250 ml
1 cup	orange juice	250 ml
1/2 cup	sugar	125 ml

1 .Grease and flour a bundt pan or tube pan. Preheat the oven to 325F (170C)

2. In a large bowl, cream together the sugar and the butter until light and fluffy.

3. Add the eggs, one at a time, beating well. Add the orange rind.

4. Stir together the flour, baking powder, and salt.

5. Add the dry mixture to the creamed mixture alternately with the milk, making three additions of dry and two of milk.

6. Spoon cake batter into prepared pan, bake at 325F(170C) for 1 1/4 to 1 1/2 hours or until knife inserted into cake comes out clean. Continued on next page

7. Let cool in pan for 5 minutes then invert onto a large plate

8. Meanwhile, in saucepan, combine orange juice and sugar; bring to a boil , stirring constantly. When sugar has dissolved, remove from heat.

9. Using a long skewer, poke lots of holes to about halfway into the cake. Gradually drizzle the warm glaze over the hot cake; do this several times, scooping up sauce. Let cool.

10. Serve with whipped cream. This cake freezes wonderfully!

LUSCIOUS GINGER CAKE WITH CRYSTALLISED GINGER CREAM FROSTING

More ginger! I love ginger, in fact I love all spices. This is a lovely two layer cake that uses stout in the cake mixture. You can also use a dark beer or if none, black tea can be substituted. The beer should be opened the night before so it will be flat when added to batter. This cake is a real stunner. Similar to a strong gingerbread. Decorated with orange slices and cranberries if desired, it is beautiful too. Cake can be made a day ahead.

21/2 cups	all purpose flour	750 ml
2 tsp	ground ginger or 1Tbsp (15 ml).fresh grated	10 ml
2 tsp	ground cinnamon	10 ml
2 tsp	baking soda	10 ml
1/2 tsp	ground cloves	3 ml
1/2 tsp	salt	3 ml
1 cup	unsalted butter, (2 sticks) room temperature	250 ml
11/4cups	(packed) golden brown sugar	300 ml
2	large eggs	
1 cup	mild-flavored (light) molasses	250 ml
3/4 cup	stout (beer), flat, room temperature or steeped black tea	175 ml

3 cups	chilled whipping cream
6 Tbsp	powdered sugar
3 Tbsp	minced crystallized ginger
	orange slices, quartered, crystallized ginger slices
	fresh cranberries

1. Preheat oven to 350F (180C). Butter and flour two 9" cake pans (1L) with 2" high sides. Continued on next page

2. Sift first six ingredients into medium bowl; set aside.

3. Using electric mixer, beat butter and brown sugar in large bowl until light and fluffy. Add eggs, one at a time, beating well after each addition. Beat in molasses.

4. Beat in flour mixture alternately with stout in 3 additions each (mixture may look curdled). Beat just until smooth. Divide batter between prepared pans; smooth tops.

5. Bake cakes until tester inserted into center comes out clean, about 40 minutes. Cool cakes in pans on rack 10 minutes. Turn cakes out onto racks; cool completely. (Can be made 1 day ahead. Wrap in plastic; let stand at room temperature.)

6. Frosting: Using electric mixer, beat cream and powdered sugar in large bowl until peaks form.

7. Fold in minced crystallized ginger.

8. Place 1 cake layer on platter. Spread 2 cups frosting over top. Top with second cake layer. Spread remaining frosting over top and sides of cake. Arrange orange slices, ginger slices and cranberries on top. (Can be made 2 hours ahead. Chill. Let stand at room temperature 20 minutes before serving.)

9. The whipped cream frosting is what makes this cake so really good!

Makes 10 servings.

CHOCOLATE ZUCCHINI CAKE

This cake is yummy unfrosted, just dusted with powdered icing sugar or topped with vanilla frosting or if you are a total chocoholic, chocolate frosting.

2 oz	unsweetened chocolate (2 squares)	50 gr
3 eggs		
1 1/4 cups	white sugar	300 ml
1 cup	vegetable oil, OR ½ oil ½ applesauce	250 ml
2 cups	zucchini, grated (or a smidge more if wanted) that the zucchini isn't too bitter	Check 500 ml
1 tsp	vanilla extract	5 ml
2 cups	all-purpose flour	500 ml
1 tsp	baking soda	5 ml
1 tsp	salt	5 ml
1 tsp	ground cinnamon	5 ml
1/2 tsp.	nutmeg (optional)	3 ml
1 cup	semisweet chocolate chips	250 ml

1. Preheat oven to 350F (180 C). grease and flour 9 x 13" 3.5 L pan or a Bundt pan.

2. In a microwave-safe bowl, microwave chocolate until melted. Stir occasionally until chocolate is smooth.

3. In a large bowl, combine eggs, sugar, oil, vanilla and chocolate. Beat well. Stir in the flour baking soda, salt and cinnamon and nutmeg if using.

4. Fold in the chocolate chips and zucchini. Pour batter into pan.

6. Bake in preheated oven for 35 minutes, or until a toothpick inserted into the center of cake comes out clean or 75 minutes in a Bundt pan but please check sooner.

CHOCOLATE ALMOND SHEET CAKE WITH CHOCOLATE SOUR CREAM FROSTING

This is a wonderful cake to whip up and take to any gathering. It feeds a crowd nicely. Add some instant coffee for a mocha flavoured cake. Also great to have on hand for lunch boxes and any friends who might drop by for a coffee! The nuts are optional.

2 cups	flour	250 ml
1 cup	sweetened instant chocolate drink mix (such as NesQuik)	250 ml
1 tsp	baking soda	5 ml
1 tsp	baking powder	5 ml
1/2 tsp	salt	3 ml
1 cup	unsalted butter, (2 sticks) room temperature	250 ml
1 1/2 cups	(packed) golden brown sugar	375 ml
3	large eggs	
11/2 cups	sour cream	375 ml
3 cups	semisweet chocolate chips (18 ounces)	750 ml
1/2 cup	almonds, toasted, chopped (optional)	125 ml

1. Preheat oven to 350F (180C). Butter and flour 13x 9x 2-inch metal baking pan (3.5L).

2. Whisk first 5 ingredients in medium bowl to blend.

3. Beat butter in large bowl until fluffy. Gradually add sugar, beating until well blended.

4. Beat in eggs 1 at a time. Beat in flour mixture in 4 additions alternately with 3/4 cup sour cream in 3 additions.

Continued on next page…

5. Fold in 11/2cups chocolate chips and almonds; spread in prepared pan. Bake cake until tester inserted into center comes out clean, about 45 minutes. Transfer to rack; cool cake.

6. Meanwhile, combine remaining 3/4 cups sour cream and 1 1/2 cups chocolate chips in heavy medium saucepan. Stir over very low heat just until chocolate melts and frosting is smooth (do not boil). Spread frosting over cake in pan. Let stand until frosting sets, at least 1 hour.

If desired you can decorate with some toasted almond flakes and chocolate shavings. For a bit of mocha flavor you can add 1/4 cup of instant coffee to the cake mixture.

CARMELIZED UPSIDE-DOWN PEAR TART

You will think you have died and gone to heaven! You can also use thinly sliced apples, or add some raisins, a bit of ginger. You can also use an aluminum pie plate if you don't have a cast iron frying pan. This is actually really easy to make!

4	Bosc pears, large firm-ripe (2 lb total)	1 kg
1/4 cup	unsalted butter (1 stick)	50 ml
1/2 cup	sugar	125 ml
1/2tsp	cinnamon	3 ml
	pastry dough, un-cooked, store bought or home made	

1. Peel and halve pears and remove the cores.

2. Heat butter in a 9- to 10-inch well-seasoned cast-iron skillet over moderate heat until foam subsides, then stir in sugar (sugar will not be dissolved).

3. Arrange pears cut sides up, in skillet with wide parts at rim of skillet. Sprinkle pears with cinnamon and cook, undisturbed, until sugar turns a deep golden caramel. (This can take as little as 10 minutes or as much as 25, depending on pears, skillets, and stove.) Don't overcook because the pears will still cook in the oven after.

4. Cool pears completely in skillet.

5. Put oven rack in middle position and preheat oven to 425°F (220C). Continued on next page

6. Roll out dough on a lightly floured surface with a floured rolling pin into a 12-inch round and trim to a 9 1/2" to 10 1/2" round. Arrange pastry over caramelized pears, tucking edge around pears inside rim of skillet.

7. Bake tart until pastry is golden brown, 30 to 35 minutes. Cool on rack 5 minutes to let sauce thicken a bit.

8. Invert a rimmed serving plate (slightly larger than skillet) over skillet and, using pot holders to hold skillet and plate tightly together, invert tart onto plate. Scary but it works!(most of the time)

9. Serve tart warm or at room temperature. With ice cream or whipped cream or au natural. Makes 8 servings.

BANANA-UPSIDE DOWN INSIDE OUT CAKE

This cake does not look pretty but it tastes fantastic!!! Serve slightly warm with whipped cream or vanilla ice-cream. If you don't have enough bananas you can substitute half the amount with crushed pineapple. Enjoy!!

1 cup	firmly packed light brown sugar	250 ml
6 Tbsp	unsalted butter, (3/4 stick softened	90 ml
2	large ripe bananas, sliced	
11/2 cups	cake flour	375 ml
3/4 tsp	baking soda	3 ml
1/2 tsp	baking powder	2 ml
1/2 tsp	salt	2 ml
1 cup	mashed ripe bananas (about 2)	250 ml
1/2 cup	buttermilk	125 ml
1 tsp	vanilla extract	5 ml
11/4 cups	sugar	300 ml
1/3 cup	vegetable shortening	75 ml
2	eggs	

1. Position rack in lowest third of oven and preheat to 350F (180C).

2. Using electric mixer, cream brown sugar and butter in medium bowl until well mixed.

3. Spread brown sugar mixture over bottom of 9-inch (1L) square baking dish with 2-inch high sides or a 10 inch round pan.

4. Arrange banana slices on top of brown sugar mixture, covering completely. Set cake pan aside. Continued on next page

5. Combine flour, baking soda, baking powder and salt in small bowl.

6. Mix mashed bananas, buttermilk and vanilla in another small bowl.

7. Using electric mixer, cream 1 1/4cups (300ml) sugar and shortening until fluffy. Add eggs 1 at a time, beating after each addition.

8. Add dry ingredients alternatively with buttermilk mixture, mixing until just combined.

9. Pour batter over bananas in pan. Bake until cake pulls away from sides of pan and tester inserted into center of cake comes out clean, about 55 minutes.

10. Transfer to rack and cool slightly. Turn cake out carefully onto plate. Serve warm or at room temperature. Whipped cream or ice cream make this cake a dream!

MAMA'S BIRTHDAY CAKE

Gloria Greenwood- This cake has been used to celebrate hundreds of birthdays! It has been passed from person to person and now from me to you. It is a never fail classic birthday pound cake. Better on the second day and delicious with ice cream.

1 cup	butter	250 ml
2 cups	sugar	500 ml
1/2cup	water	125 ml
1/2cup	milk	125 ml
1 tsp.	baking powder	5 ml
1/2tsp.	salt	2 ml
3 cups	flour	750 ml
4	eggs	
11/2 tsp.	lemon extract	7 ml

1. Grease and flour a tube pan and preheat oven to 350F (180C).

2. In a large bowl, cream together the butter and sugar.

3. Add milk and water and beat well.

4. In a separate bowl, mix together the flour, salt and baking powder.

5. To the creamed mixture add 1 cup of the dry mixture..

6. Next, beat in one egg.

7. Beat in another cup of flour mixture.

8. Beat in another egg.

9. Beat in the final cup of flour mixture.

Continued on next page

MAMA'S BIRTHDAY CAKE Continued

10. Beat in the last two eggs.

11. Add the lemon extract.

12. Bake for one hour or until toothpick comes clean and sides come away from pan.

13. Cool and frost with your best buttercream icing. A touch of almond flavoring in the icing is nice with this cake.

BLACKBERRY CAKE WITH CARAMEL ICING

A lovely summer cake made with freshly picked wild blackberries. You could also use raspberries. The old fashioned fudge like frosting is delicious! Decorate with some pansies.

1 tsp.	baking soda	5 ml
1 cup	buttermilk	250 ml
1 cup	butter,softened	250 ml
2 cups	sugar	500 ml
1 tsp.	cinnamon	5 ml
1 tsp	nutmeg	5 ml
1 tsp.	salt	5 ml
3	eggs	
3 cups	flour	750 ml
1 cup	blackberries, drained and kept as whole as possible.	250 ml

1. Dissolve the baking soda in the buttermilk.

2. Then mix everything together, adding the blackberries last.

3. Bake in 2 greased and floured, 8" or 9" (1L) layer pans at 350F (180C) for approx. 35 minutes

CARAMEL ICING

1 cup	brown sugar	250 ml
1/2cup	white sugar	125 ml
1/3cup	milk	75 ml
2 Tbsp	shortening	30 ml
2 Tbsp	butter	30 ml
1/2 tsp.	salt	2 ml
1 tsp.	vanilla	5 ml

Continued on next page

1. In a saucepan, bring ingredients to a boil and cook for 1 minute.
2. Cool to lukewarm and beat until the correct consistency for spreading on the cake.

QUICK MANDARIN CAKE WITH BROWN SUGAR GLAZE

Need something in a hurry? Need something yummy?

1 cup	flour	250 ml
1 cup	sugar	250 ml
1 tsp.	baking soda	5 ml
1/2 tsp.	salt	2 ml
1	egg	
10 oz.	mandarin oranges, canned, drained	284 ml
3/4 cup	brown sugar	175 ml
3 Tbsp.	butter	45 ml
3 Tbsp.	milk	45 ml
1 tsp.	grated orange rind (optional)	5 ml

1. Preheat oven to 350F(180C)

2. Put first six ingredients in a bowl and beat for 3 minutes at medium speed until smooth.

3. Pour into a greased 8" square pan. Bake at 350 F (180C) for 30-40 mins.

4. Combine glaze ingredients in a saucepan and bring to a boil, stirring constantly. As soon as cake comes out of oven, pour the glaze over it. Return to the oven and cook 2 minutes more. If you prefer it less sweet, only use 2/3 of the glaze.

BLUEBERRY ORANGE CAKE

Topped with a light orange glaze, this wonderful cake is summer all year round. Garnish with fresh blueberries and orange peel twists. It can also be made with a lemon glaze.

3/4 cup	butter	175 ml
1 cup	sugar	250 ml
3	eggs	
1 tsp.	vanilla	5 ml
2 cups	flour	500ml
1 1/2 tsp.	baking powder	7 ml
3/4 cup	milk	175 ml
2 cups	blueberries (fresh or frozen)	500 ml
2 Tbsp.	flour	30 ml
3 Tbsp.	frozen orange juice concentrate or lemonade concentrate	45 ml
1 cup	icing sugar	250 ml

1. Grease a 10" tube pan or bundt and dust with flour. Preheat oven to 350F (180C).

2. In large bowl, cream sugar and butter. Add eggs and beat well. Add vanilla.

3. Sift together dry ingredients and add to creamed mixture alternating with milk. Mix only until blended.

4. Toss berries in 2 Tbsp. flour and fold into batter.

5. Spoon cake into pan. Bake for 50-55 minutes or until toothpick comes out clean or firm to the touch. Let cake rest 10 minutes then turn out.

6. For Glaze: Mix together the orange concentrate and icing sugar. Pour over warm cake and let soak in. Prick cake a few times first to let some glaze sink in.

APPLE MOLASSES CAKE

Edna Boudreau -This recipe has been passed down through four generations in the Boudreau family. Similar to a gingerbread, it is a Cape Breton classic. Serve like an upside down cake and pass the ice cream! It can also be made without the apples.

1 cup	shortening or butter	250 ml
1 cup	brown sugar	250 ml
1 cup	molasses	250 ml
1	egg	
1 cup	steeped boiled tea	250 ml
1 tsp.	baking soda	5 ml
3 cups	flour	750 ml
1 tsp.	each, nutmeg, cinnamon, allspice, salt	5 ml
1/2 cups	sugar	~~500~~ ml
7	apples, peeled and sliced	

1. Grease 9 x 13" (1L) pan. Preheat oven to 350F(180C).

2. In large bowl, beat together the first four ingredients.

3. In a separate bowl, mix together the tea and baking soda. It will foam.

4. Add the tea mixture to the creamed mixture. Stir with a wooden spoon.

5. Add the flour and spices. Mix well.

6. Cover the bottom of the pan with the peeled and sliced apples. They should be four layers thick. Sprinkle with the sugar and pour batter over.

7. Bake for 50 -55 minutes.

1, 2, 3 PEANUT BUTTER COOKIES (Flourless)

I got this recipe off the Internet and they are ridiculously simple to make ! My daughter loves to make these.

1 cup	sugar (3/4 cup (75ml) if you want)	250 ml
1	large egg	
1 cup	peanut butter (crunchy or smooth)	250 ml

1. Combine sugar and egg in mixing bowl, stirring until smooth Add peanut butter and mix in thoroughly.

2. Roll into walnut-sized balls and place on ungreased cookie sheets at least 2" apart.

3. Flatten with the tines of a fork. Turn 90 degrees and flatten with fork again to create cross hatches.

4. Bake 10 minutes at 375F (190C) or until done. Cool in pan for 1 minute before removing to cooling rack.

NO FAIL FUDGE

3 cups	semi sweet chocolate chips (18oz)	750 ml
1 can	sweetened Condensed Milk(14 oz)	397 ml
	dash of salt	
11/2 tsp	vanilla extract	7 ml

1. In heavy pot, over low heat, melt chocolate with salt and condensed milk.

2. Remove from heat, stir in ½ cup (125ml) nuts if desired and spread into waxpaper lined 8 or 9"pan.

3. Chill two hours. Peel off paper and cut into squares. Refrigerate.

CHOCO MOCHA TRUFFLE COOKIES

These are soft on the inside and crispy on the outside. Very chocolatey, is there such a word?

1/2 cups	butter	500 ml
1/2 cups	semisweet chocolate pieces	500 ml
1 Tbsp.	instant coffee crystals	15 ml
3/4 cup	sugar	175 ml
3/4 cup	brown sugar	175 ml
2	eggs	
2 tsp.	vanilla	10 ml
2 cups	flour	500 ml
1/3 cup	unsweetened cocoa powder	75 ml
2 tsp.	baking powder	10 ml
1/4 tsp.	salt	1 ml
1 cup	semisweet chocolate chips	250 ml

1. Preheat oven to 350F (180C).

2. In a saucepan, melt the butter and 1/2 cups of chocolate pieces over low heat.

3. Remove from the heat and add the coffee, stir and then cool for 5 minutes.

4. Stir in the white sugar, brown sugar, eggs and vanilla.

5. In a medium sized bowl, stir together the flour, cocoa powder, baking powder and salt.

6. Stir the flour mixture into the coffee mixture. Add the one cup of chocolate chips and stir.

8. Drop dough by rounded tablespoons onto a lightly greased baking sheet and bake for 10 minutes. Let cool for a minute before removing from sheet. Makes 30 cookies.

RAISIN MOLASSES GEMS

Debra Morris -These are the favourite cookies of a neighbor of Debra, whenever she makes them she has to make more if he's anywhere near! They flatten during baking giving an interesting cracked top.

3/4 cup	shortening	175 ml
1 cup	sugar	250 ml
1/4 cup	molasses	50 ml
1	egg	
2 cups	flour	500 ml
2 tsp.	baking soda	10 ml
1 tsp.	cinnamon	5 ml
1/2 tsp.	each, ground cloves, and ginger	2 ml
1/4 tsp.	salt	1 ml
1 cup	raisins	250 ml

1. In a large bowl, cream together the shortening and sugar until light and fluffy.

2. Add the molasses and egg, mixing well.

3. Combine the dry ingredients except raisins and add to the creamed mixture.

4. Stir in the raisins.

5. If desired, cover and let chill about 1 hour.

6. Shape the dough into 1" balls and roll in sugar to coat.

7. Place on cookie sheet with enough room for cookies to spread.

8. Bake at 350F(180C) for 10-12 minutes.

FROSTED MOLASSES LOLLIPOP COOKIES

Joanne Duffett - Kids just love these. They are always the first thing to disappear at any bake sale.

1/2 cup	margarine	125 ml
1/2cup	sugar	125 ml
1	egg	
2 Tbsp.	water	30 ml
1/2 cup	molasses	125 ml
2 1/2 cup	flour	625 ml
1/4 tsp.	salt	1 ml
1 tsp.	baking soda	5 ml
1 Tbsp.	cinnamon	5 ml

White frosting tinted with different colours (or just white)
Chocolate chips for eyes and noses
Popsicle sticks for handles

1. Preheat oven to 350F (180C)

2. Cream together the margarine, sugar, egg, water and molasses.

3. Mix together the dry ingredients and add to the rest stirring with a wooden spoon. It will be stiff.

4. Take a tablespoon of dough and roll into a ball. Place on cookie sheet and flatten a bit. Insert popsicle stick like a sucker.

5. Bake for 8-10 minutes and take out and cool.

6. Spread each cookie with frosting and use two chips for eyes, one for a nose and make the mouth with the edge of a knife or more chips if wanted

CHOCOLATE, PEANUT BUTTER, RAISIN, OATMEAL COOKIES

No flour needed! These are large tasty cookies. Great for a hike.

2 cups	butter, softened	500 ml
11/2cup	sugar	375 ml
11/2cup	brown sugar, firmly packed	375 ml
4	eggs	
1 tsp.	vanilla extract	5 ml
2 cups	peanut butter	500 ml
6 cups	rolled oats	1.5L
2 1/2 tsp.	baking soda	12 ml
1 cup	chocolate chips	250 ml
1 cup	raisins	250 ml

1. Preheat oven to 350F(180C)

2. Cream together the butter and both sugars

3. Add the eggs, one at a time, beating well after each addition.

4. Mix in the vanilla, peanut butter, oats, baking soda, chocolate chips and raisins. Blend well.

5. Drop rounded spoonfuls on a greased cookie sheet and bake for 10 -12 minutes or until light brown. Cool and serve. Makes 6-8 dozen.

CRANBERRY OATMEAL WHITE CHOCOLATE CHIP COOKIES

These are really great! Good snacking cookies. Take to a picnic!

2/3 cup	butter, softened	150 ml
2/3 cup	brown sugar, packed	150 ml
2	eggs	
1 1/2 cups	rolled oats	375 ml
1 1/2 cups	flour	375 ml
1 tsp	baking soda	5 ml
1/2tsp	salt	2 ml
6oz	dried cranberries	170 gr
2/3cup	white chocolate chips or chunks	150 ml

1. Preheat oven to 375F (190C)

2. In a medium bowl, beat together the butter and sugar until light and fluffy. Add eggs, mixing well.

3. In a separate bowl, combine the oats, flour, salt and baking powder. Add this to the creamed butter mixture in a few additions. Mixing well.

4. Stir in the cranberries and the chocolate.(You can use regular chocolate chips if white is not available.)

5. Drop by rounded Tablespoons (15ml) onto ungreased cookie sheets. They will spread a bit as they cook. Bake for 10 minutes at 375F(190C) until light golden brown. Makes 2 doz. large cookies.

DEVIL'S FOOD SNAPS

Louise Boudreau - These are crunchy and light, a good cookie for dunking in coffee or tea. They freeze well.

2 cups	sugar	500 ml
1 cup	brown sugar (packed)	250 ml
11/2cup	butter (softened)	375 ml
6 oz.	unsweetened chocolate, melted and cooled	175 ml
2 tsp.	vanilla	10 ml
3	eggs	
4 cups	flour	1 L
1 tsp.	baking soda	5 ml
2 tsp.	baking powder	10 ml
1 tsp.	salt	5 ml

1. Combine the sugars and margarine. Beat until light and fluffy.

2. Add the chocolate, vanilla, food color, and eggs, beat well.

3. Add the flour, baking soda and baking powder and salt, mix well.

4. Cover and chill for 20 minutes.

5. Heat oven to 350F (180C) Lightly grease cookie sheets. Shape dough into 1" balls and roll in sugar to coat. Place 3" apart on sheet.

6. Bake at 350F (180C) for 15 minutes. Cookies will puff up and flatten during baking. Cool 1 minute and remove from sheet. (4 doz. cookies)

PUMPKIN CHEESE CAKE

I won this cake in a raffle many years ago and it was so delicious I had to track down the cook and get the recipe. Here it is!

1 1/4 cup	gingersnap cookies (20 x 2" cookies)	
1/4 cup	butter, melted	50 ml
3 pkgs.	cream cheese (8 oz. each)	750 gr
1 tsp.	cinnamon	5 ml
1 tsp.	ginger	5 ml
2 tsp.	ground cloves	10 ml
1 can	pumpkin (16 oz.)	500 gr
4	eggs	
1 cup	sugar	250 ml

1. Preheat oven to 350F(180C).

2. Mix together the crumbs and butter and press into a 9 x 3 (1L) springform pan. Bake 10 minutes. Cool.

3. Reduce oven temperature to 300F (160C).

4. In a large bowl, beat together cream cheese, 1 cup sugar, and spices at medium speed until smooth and fluffy.

5. Add pumpkin. Add eggs, one at a time, beating at low speed.

6. Pour over crumb mixture and bake for 1 1/4 hours approx. until centre is firm.

7. Cover and refrigerate at least 3 hours before serving and no longer than 48 hours. Serve with whipped cream for an extra touch. Serves 12.

FASTEST CHEESECAKE IN THE WORLD

This is a simple and wonderful cheese cake. More of a pie actually but cheesecake style. If you have all the ingredients you can put it together in under 5 minutes! It does take an hour to firm. My mother's mother used to make this.

1 can	sweetened condensed milk	397 ml
8 oz	. package cream cheese (no fat won't work)	250 gr
1/3 cup	lemon juice	75 ml
1 tsp	vanilla	5 ml
1 can	cherry pie filling, or blueberry	
1	graham cracker pie crust (the large one works well; if you use the smaller one you'll have lots of extra topping when you 'lick' the bowl)	

1. Put the first four ingredients into a food processor or blender and mix until there are no lumps of cream cheese left. Pour it into the crust

2. Spread the the pie filling on top. If you'd rather, you can use fresh fruit slices or canned fruit slices or berries of any kind.

3. Chill for about an hour. (It'll take that long to want some more after you eat what's left over when you clean the bowl!)

4. To be really decadent, top with whipped cream and a mint leaf.

CITY SARAH'S BUTTER TARTS

Sarah Lynk – A real Canadian treat. These are the best butter tarts I've eaten and Sarah is one of the best cooks I know! Her house is always full of wonderful smells and there is always something delicious to eat.

1/3 cup	butter	80 ml
1/2cup	golden corn syrup	125 ml
1/2cup	brown sugar	125 ml
2/3 cup	raisins and or pecans	150 ml
2	eggs, beaten lightly	
	pastry , homemade is best	

1. Grease a tart pan or shallow muffin pan with 3 "(8cm) cups

2. Roll out the pastry and cut into rounds to fit the pan. You can use a glass upside down.

3. In a heavy saucepan, melt the butter, and stir in the syrup and brown sugar. Set aside to cool.

4. Fold in the beaten eggs until combined and then add the raisins(pecans). Pour into the prepared tart shells.

5. Bake in the center of the oven at 450F (230C) for 15 minutes Remove from the oven and loosen the sides with a sharp knife. Let cool on rack for 10 minutes before taking out of the pan.

COFFEE COCONUT CREAM PIE

Carolyn Bourque - A light and refreshing dessert. Say no to the after dinner coffee and have this instead!

1 envelope	gelatin, unflavored
2 cups	sugar
1 cup	coffee, freshly brewed
11/4 cup	toasted coconut
1 tsp.	vanilla
2 cups	whipping cream
1	9" pastry pie shell, cooked or graham crumb pie shell

1. Mix together the gelatin and sugar in a small saucepan.

2. Add the hot coffee and stir over medium heat until granules are dissolved.

3. Pour into a large bowl and add the vanilla and 1 cup of the coconut.

4. Chill, stirring occasionally until the mixture thickens to the consistency of unbeaten egg white.

5. Beat 1 cup of whipping cream until stiff peaks form. Gently fold into the coffee mixture.

6. Pour into the prepared pie shell and refrigerate until set. (Approx.1 hour).

7. Whip the remaining cream and spread over the pie. Garnish with 1/4 cup of coconut. Serves 5 - 6.

RHUBARB CUSTARD PIE

Mary White – Another terrific cook! This is a really delicious pie.
A real Spring favourite. With a golden tipped fluffy meringue
topping who can resist?

1	baked and cooled 9" pie shell	1 L
3 cups	rhubarb, chopped	750 ml
5	eggs, separated	5
1 Tbsp.	grated orange rind (optional)	15 ml
1 1/2 cups	sugar	375 ml
1 1/2 Tbsp.	butter	22 ml
1 1/2 Tbsp.	cornstarch	22 ml

1. Cook rhubarb in top of double boiler until soft.

2. Mix sugar and cornstarch together and add to rhubarb. Stir
   and cook 1 minute. Add the butter.

3. Beat the egg yolks and fold into rhubarb mixture. Add orange
if using .Cook for another 5 minutes until thickened.

4. Cool slightly and pour into pie shell.

5. Top with meringue and bake at 400F(200C) until golden
   brown.

MERINGUE: Beat egg whites until stiff and add 8 Tbsp (120ml)
sugar while still beating. Mound on top of pie spreading to
edges.

BREEZY BLUEBERRY MAPLE PIE

Throw away all your old blueberry pie recipes! Simple and delicious but not too sweet. The maple syrup is what gives it that special something. Add 1/2 cup of cranberries or black berries for some extra oomph! Serve with a good vanilla ice-cream

4 cups	fresh blueberries (about 23 ounces) or frozen	1L
1 cup	pure maple syrup	250 ml
1/4 cup	unbleached all purpose flour	50 ml
1/4 cup	quick-cooking tapioca (or corn starch in a pinch but tapioca is better)	50 ml
5 tsp	fresh lemon juice	25 ml
	prepared pie dough for top and bottom	

1. Place baking sheet on bottom of oven and position rack in center; preheat to 375F (190C).

2. Combine blueberries, (1/2 cup (125ml) cranberries or blackberries if using) syrup, flour, tapioca and juice in bowl; toss to blend Let stand 15 minutes. (If you like a sweeter pie, add 1/2 cup (125ml) sugar.)

3. Roll out dough on floured surface to 12-inch round. Transfer to 9-inch-diameter glass pie dish.

4. Pour filling into crust. Roll out second dough disk on floured surface to 12-inch round. Arrange over filling. Seal crusts at edge of dish. Trim overhang to 3/4 inch; fold under and crimp edge decoratively. Using small knife, cut several slits in top crust.

5. Bake pie until juices bubble thickly and crust is golden, about 1 hour. Cool pie on rack. Serve at room temperature. Serves 6 to 8.

CAMPING PANCAKES

Cathy Cameron- Last but not least, I wanted to include these so I wouldn't have to find the piece of paper I have this recipe written on, every time I make them! We have had these many times in many places and they are always gobbled up instantly! To take camping, just mix the dry ingredients in a zip lock baggie.

1 1/4cup	all-purpose flour	300 ml
2 Tbsp.	sugar	30 ml
2 tsp.	baking powder	10 ml
1/2 tsp.	salt	2 ml
1	egg, beaten	
1 cup	milk	250 ml
1 Tbsp.	cooking oil	15 ml

1. Stir together the flour, sugar, baking powder and salt.

2. Combine the egg, oil and milk. Add it to the dry mixture all at once. Stir until blended but still a bit lumpy.

3. Pour about 1/4 cup (50ml) batter onto a hot griddle or skillet for a standard sized pancake or 1Tbsp.(15 ml) for a dollar sized pancake.

4. Cook until the top of the pancake has a bubbly surface and slightly dry edges and the underside is golden, flip and cook until bottom golden. (Second side cooks faster)

5. Serve with real maple syrup! Makes about 8 four inch pancakes or 30 dollar sized.

Until next time!

www.DuffettFolkArt.com

Drop by for a visit….

ISBN 141202802-7